Say This of Horses

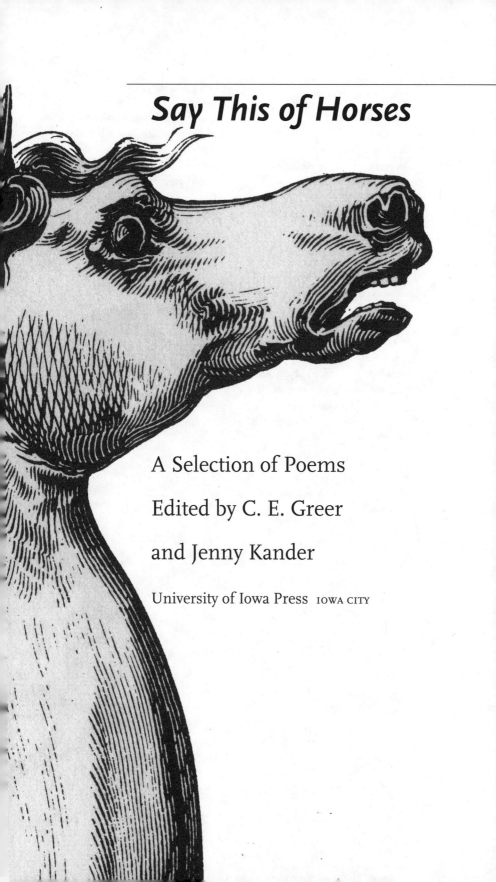

Say This of Horses

A Selection of Poems

Edited by C. E. Greer

and Jenny Kander

University of Iowa Press IOWA CITY

University of Iowa Press,
Iowa City 52242
http://www.uiowapress.org
Copyright © 2007 by the
University of Iowa Press
All rights reserved
Printed in the United States of America

Design by Richard Hendel

The University of Iowa Press is a
member of Green Press Initiative and
is committed to preserving natural
resources.

Grateful acknowledgment is made
to the following offices of Indiana
University, Bloomington, for the
generous support of this book: the Office
of the Chancellor, the Office of the Vice
President for Research, and the College
Arts and Humanities Institute.

Printed on acid-free paper

Lccn: 2006932731

ISBN-10: 1-58729-526-1

ISBN-13: 978-1-58729-526-3

07 08 09 10 11 P 5 4 3 2 1

To Sue, Genevieve, Dirk,
and riding into the woods.

To Oren, Ella, and Natalia—
finding what you love to do
and doing it well
will bring you joy.

Homme vous trouverez ici une nouvelle représentation de l'univers...

tout terriblement

Guillaume Apollinaire

Contents

This well-researched and commodious anthology opens with a reproduction of Guillaume Apollinaire's charming horse calligram, includes poets as disparate as Henry Wadsworth Longfellow and Lawrence Ferlinghetti, and treats the reader to May Swenson's "Bronco Busting, Event #1," James Wright's "A Blessing," and other familiar poems.

I am flattered to be represented in this ambitious compendium of horse poems that ranges so widely every taste will be gratified. Indeed, I can imagine readers poring over the table of contents in search, say, of Wallace Stevens's aristocratic "Polo Ponies Practicing" or Donald Hall's justly famous "Names of Horses."

Yes, the horse has been a symbol of power and flight down the ages. The horse has been our enduring myth, the repository for our love and terror. The horse has been cruelly used and tenderly worshipped—and never, to my knowledge, have poems celebrating its existence been anthologized with the degree of intellectual probity and earthy passion that *Say This of Horses* exhibits.

The horse has been a powerful presence through every phase of human experience. Early peoples hunted horses for food and in later millennia domesticated their descendants for war and work in agrarian civilizations. As those roles have been eclipsed in modern times, the horse has democratized certain experiences limited in the past to society's most privileged classes. Today, by providing recreation and leisure, the horse helps us escape from our technological age to those moments of existential awareness afforded by animal companions.

And also now the horse retains its power in cultural memory, that composite of human experience in our collective consciousness and imagination. Along with lion as symbol for predator, stag for wild prey, and ox for servile beast, the horse is a primal emblem of controllable but unbroken spirit—with all the associations of that word's Latin root, *spiritus*. Even without the experience ourselves, we comprehend how early hunters would invoke the animal's spirit in their mutual striving, their intertwining roles in the life-death mystery. We understand how the horses of charioteers and mounted warriors were spiritual as well as physical comrades in the terror of mortal contest, and how laborers in those societies could worship this animal for its strength and endurance in their mundane work. It is not surprising that these animals often serve to epitomize, even magnify, the aspirations and disappointments of our competitions now.

And we recognize a nobility in the horse's retention of spirit through the changes and the vagaries of life's condition. It is a nobility celebrated and preserved in art from the time when early peoples painted horses on cave walls and etched them on rock surfaces to their depiction in sculpture and relief, painting and literature, from all civilizations in which the horse was known.

The idea for this anthology germinated through our increasing encounters with *Equus* as a presence in poetry. Research for a collection of this kind turned up nothing of the sort we envisioned, and it confirmed our sense of the need for this volume. With a notable exception or two, the reader seeking poetry focused on horses must go to local publications or those of special thematic interest, such as western or cowboy poetry, which present the horse as one element in a particular way of life. And none incorporates the scope of time, place, or themes represented in the large body of work that exists. Nor does any offer verse of consistently high quality or appeal to the range of both poetry and horse lovers.

We began with a survey of all poetry available in English and English translation. Our primary criterion for selection was quality of poetic evocation. Beyond that we sought to represent a wide range of epochs and nationalities. The horse or one of its qualities had to be the focus of the poem. Variety of poetic form and style was also desirable but not at the expense of high-quality verse. The process gave us 230 poems we would love to see together between book covers. The realities of book production, however, and of obtaining permission helped us distill the works to the exciting collection in your hands. These represent writers from twenty-two nationalities, including poets whose names will be recognizable in a regional context as well as those familiar nationally and internationally.

The structure of the book was provided by a set of six themes that emerged from this body of work itself. These categories, taken together, provide a fascinating view into how varieties of experience are refracted in poetry—a kind of epistemological prism for the ways we know about something as complex as the human relationship with the horse.

The first section, Antiquity, illustrates knowledge transmitted through millennia by what we call folklore in the broadest sense. The experience of preliterate peoples is manifest physically now only in funerary materials, cave paintings, petroglyphs, or other artifacts. Yet these convey their visceral tie with horses so effectively that poets such as Henry Wadsworth Longfellow and Theodore Enslin evoke the mystical rituals that bound such groups before blood relationships with animals had become blood sports. By the time of early literate traditions, an animal's *spiritus* included association with elements of the cosmos critical to society as well as relevant figures in the pantheon. Such associations are echoed for our times by poets such as Pattiann Rogers and Tess Gallagher, who ascribe to horses different but comparable modern powers.

Within the second theme, Here, Now, are expressions from those who encounter the immediate, physical equine presence. The universal appreciation for its raw physicality is reflected in a paean to the chariot horse from ancient Ireland. Recent poets such as Leslie Ullman, Lawrence Ferlinghetti, and William Hathaway capture moments when the physical encounter inspires earthy awe, humor, and exhilaration. The power of experience in the work of veterinarians and ferriers is provided by Michael List and David Baker. And finally, the magnification horses give to the emotions we have for aging and death is the subject of Donald Hall's remembrance for the generations that toiled with humankind, of Maxine Kumin's drawing of association with our own mortality, and of Yusef Komunyakaa's depiction of a helpless horse dying in terrible circumstances.

Beyond the physical form of the horse are metaphysical qualities, the subject of poems in Essence, the book's third section. These are qualities we sense and the poet brings to the page from the kind of knowing we call intuition. They are essential as in the Latin *esse*, "being," which resonates for poets such as James Wright, David Wagoner, and Vachel Lindsay in a moment of contact with the animal and for others in observing their rhythm, singly or in groups. It is a spiritual moment from which Pablo Neruda will "never forget the light of the horses" or perhaps of such transcendence that Rainer Maria Rilke finds a link with Orpheus and Claude Wilkinson can image the apocalyptic horses in the Book of Revelation.

Harnessed, the fourth thematic section, incorporates poems on the horse in war, at work, and in sport or recreation. Here the knowledge is collective social experience from the time of herding and warring peoples of the steppe grasslands to our own epoch. The feelings of awe, pride, and spiritual power that the horse gave the warrior are shown in examples from early Arabian conquerors and a nineteenth-century British imperialist. As the twentieth century was the historical moment of horses being replaced by machines, the twilight of their military use in World War I produces different feelings. Their concurrent eclipse in menial work is memorialized by William Carlos Williams's spare portrait; their precarious balance on the edges of industrial urbanization is presented by Paul Zech; and a dramatic example of the useful ways that horses once were trained is given by Linda Bierds. The spread of equine activities into the greater leisure of late industrial society produces poems such as those we include on pastimes ranging from racing and polo to driving, pulling, and rodeo contests as well as informal and family recreation.

In the fifth section, Mirrors, the horse is used to shape, hold, or elaborate meanings we might not see except as reflected by something not necessarily connected by logic. Writers such as Joy Harjo modernize Native American weavings of the horse symbol with cosmic forces, while for others in our psychological age the symbol stands for complicated human relationships or for comment on political life. In the metacreative practice of writing on an experience of art appreciation, imaginative takes are presented on horses encountered in painting, collage, and carousel animals.

In the final section, Lenses, *Equus* appears at the edges of imagination where dreams and fantasies flicker and surreal images concretize. Various visions bring to Nancy Willard the twin embodiments of "Never Tame Me" and the "Keeper of Lights" and to several other poets variations of escape. W. S. Merwin finds a puzzling legend and James Dickey a kaleidoscope. Pattiann Rogers asks of her boys on ponies, "who cares if they are real or not," while Mihai Ursachi has a horse in the heart of silence bring "the news for which you have waited so long."

Many facets of the horse in poetry show this most durable companion's quality of spirit, which is malleable but so hard to break. Abstracted in symbols and visions that inspire us, it is a splendid presence to which we aspire, a nobility accessible whether we seek it in the pasture, in the paddock, or on the page, through what George Eliot calls poetry's chief energy in the "force of imagination that pierces or exalts the solid fact."

I. ANTIQUITY

. . . hooves of the gray wind forever
Thundering, . . .
—W. S. Merwin, "Two Horses"

Blood
history of the word
goes back to
"hross"
Icelandic
for the scalds
and makers of
sagas—
survives in
our pronunciation
(North New England)
                    as
"hoss."
What does not
come through:
The sacrificial eating
in those times
when blood
was smeared on arm rings
                      and
a man rode far
to carry out
his own blood sentence—
rode back with
weirgild
that his race
survive.

The figure of a man
astride his horse
above a fjord
remains
our consciousness—
a heritage as
measured out
in blood.

        Theodore Enslin

Before, a dark-haired virgin train
Chanted the death dirge of the slain;
Behind, the long procession came
Of hoary men and chiefs of fame,
With heavy hearts, and eyes of grief,
Leading the war-horse of their chief.

Stripped of his proud and martial dress,
Uncurbed, unreined, and riderless,
With darting eye, and nostril spread,
And heavy and impatient tread,
He came; and oft that eye so proud
Asked for his rider in the crowd.

They buried the dark chief; they freed
Beside the grave his battle steed;
And swift an arrow cleaved its way
To his stern heart! One piercing neigh
Arose, and, on the dead man's plain,
The rider grasps his steed again.

Henry Wadsworth Longfellow

Whitehorse, Yukon Territory . . . a horse found this fall near the Alaska border . . .
is one of the best-preserved Ice Age animals discovered in North America. The dark
chestnut hide is complete with blond mane and tail. Also recovered were a right foreleg
with the flesh remaining, a couple of bones and stomach contents. Archaeologist Ruth
Gotthardt said . . . the carcass was so well-preserved that it still smelled strongly of
dead horse.
—Boston Globe, December 25, 1993

The archaeologist is elated.
Out of the creek where it drank
its last, out of the overhanging bank
that collapsed in one fell shrug of earth,
grass, broken flowers, worms,
the ghost of Whitehorse returns.

That he was beautiful surprises
no one. Twenty-six thousand years
ago he lowered his tow-head
poised a hoof against the tide's
insistent rub. Now his bones rest
in a velvet box every bit as black

as the silt that preserved
them. Though his hide,
his tail, even his last meal,
were rescued from the soil,
what could not be conveyed
from the ancient bed was what

Whitehorse kept—over millennia
of frost, gales, northern lights—
to himself. Whitehorse steps back into
time wrapped in his inimitable death,
his presence in this newer landscape
as lingering, as singular,

as it was in life.

Jean Monahan

Oh in whose grove have we wakened, the bees
Still droning under the carved wall, the fountain playing
Softly to itself, and the gold light, muted,
Moving long over the olives; and whose,
Stamping the shadowy grass at the end of the garden,
Are these two wild horses tethered improbably
To the withes of a young quince? No rider
Is to be seen; they bear neither saddle nor bridle;
Their brute hooves splash the knee-high green
Without sound, and their flexed tails like flags float,
Whipping, their brows down like bulls. Yet the small tree
Is not shaken; and the broken arches
Of their necks in the dim air are silent
As the doorways of ruins. Birds flit in the garden:
Jay and oriole, blades in the hanging shadows,
Small cries confused. And dawn would be eastward
Over the dark neck a red mane tossed high
Like flame, and the dust brightening along the wall.
These have come up from Egypt, from the dawn countries,
Syria, and the land between the rivers,
Have ridden at the beaks of vessels, by Troy neighed,
And along the valley of the Danube, and to Etruria;
And all dust was of their making; and passion
Under their hooves puffed into flight like a sparrow
And died down when they departed. The haze of summer
Blows south over the garden terraces,
Vague through the afternoon, remembering rain;
But in the night green with beasts as April with grass
Orion would hunt high from southward, over the hill,
And the blood of beasts herald morning. Where these have passed,
Tramping white roads, their ears drinking the sword-crash,
The chariots are broken, bright battle-cars
Shambles under earth; whether by sharp bronze
Or the years' ebbing, all blood has flowed into the ground;
There was wailing at sundown, mourning for kings,
Weeping of widows, but these were faint, were forgotten,
And the columns have fallen like shadows. Crickets

Sing under the stones; and beyond the carved wall
Westward, fires drifting in darkness like the tails
Of jackals flaring, no hounds heard at their hunting,
Float outward into the dark. And these horses stamp
Before us now in this garden; and northward
Beyond the terraces the misted sea
Swirls endless, hooves of the gray wind forever
Thundering, churning the ragged spume-dusk
High that there be no horizons nor stars, and there
Are white islands riding, ghost-guarded, twisted waves flashing,
Porpoises plunging like the necks of horses.

W. S. Merwin

"What is the cause of thy journey or thy story?"

The cause of my journey and my story
The men of Erin, yonder, as we see them,
Coming towards you on the plain.
  The chariot on which is the fold, figured and cerulean,
Which is made strongly, handy, solid;
Where were active, and where were vigorous;
And where were full-wise, the noble hearted folk;
In the prolific, faithful city;—
Fine, hard, stone-bedecked, well-shafted;
Four large-chested horses in that splendid chariot;
Comely, frolicsome.

"What do we see in that chariot?"

The white-bellied, white-haired, small-eared,
Thin-sided, thin-hoofed, horse-large, steed-large horses;
With fine, shining, polished bridles;
Like a gem; or like red sparkling fire;—
Like the motion of a fawn, wounded;
Like the rustling of a loud wind in winter;—
Coming to you in that chariot.—

"What do we see in that chariot?"

We see in that chariot,
The strong, broad-chested, nimble, gray horses,—
So mighty, so broad-chested, so fleet, so choice;—
Which would wrench the sea skerries from the rocks.—
The lively, shielded, powerful horses;—
So mettlesome, so active, so clear-shining;—
Like the talon of an eagle 'gainst a fierce beast;
Which are called the beautiful Large-Gray—
The fond, large Meactroigh.

"What do we see in that chariot?"

We see in that chariot,
The horses; which are white-headed, white-hoofed, slender-legged,

Fine-haired, sturdy, imperious;
Satin-bannered, wide-chested;
Small-aged, small-haired, small-eared,
Large-hearted, large-shaped, large-nostriled;
Slender-waisted, long-bodied,—and they are foal-like;
Handsome, playful, brilliant, wild-leaping;
Which are called the Dubh-Seimhlinn.

"Who sits in that chariot?"

He who sits in that chariot,
Is the warrior, able, powerful, well-worded,
Polished, brilliant, very graceful.—
There are seven sights on his eye;
And we think that that is good vision to him;
There are six bony, fat fingers,
On each hand that comes from his shoulder;
There are seven kinds of fair hair on his head;—
Brown hair next his head's skin,
And smooth red hair over that;
And fair-yellow hair, of the colour of gold;
And clasps on the top, holding it fast;—
Whose name is Cuchullin, Seimh-suailte,
Son of Aodh, son of Agh, son of other Aodh.—
His face is like red sparkles;—
Fast-moving on the plain like mountain fleet-mist;
Or like the speed of a hill hind;
Or like a hare on rented level ground.—
It was a frequent step—a fast step—a joyful step;—
The horses coming towards us:—
Like snow hewing the slopes;—
The panting and the snorting,
Of the horses coming towards thee.

from the ancient Erse legend of Cuchullin

Some say there are wild white ponies
Being washed clean in a clear pool
Beneath a narrow falls in the middle
Of the deciduous forest existing
At the center of the sun.

Some say the thrashing of those ponies
Straining against their bridles, the water flying
From their stamping hooves in fiery pieces
And streaks rising higher than the sandbar willows
Along the bank, drops whirling like sparks
From the manes of their shaking heads,
And the shouting and splashing of the boys
Yanked off their feet by the ponies
As they attempt to wash the great shoulders
And rumps of those rearing beasts, as they lather
Their necks and breasts, stroking them,
Soothing them—all this is the source
Of the fierce binding and releasing energy
Existing at the core of the sun.

The purple jays, mad with the chaos,
Shrieking in the tops of the planetrees,
The rough-winged swallows swerving back
And forth in distress, the struggle of the boys
To soap the inner haunch, to reach
Beneath the belly, to dodge the sharp
Pawing hooves, the wide-eyed screaming
Of the slipping ponies being maneuvered
For the final rinse under the splattering falls—
All the fury of this frightening drama,
Some believe, is contained and borne steadily
Across the blue sky strictly by the startling
Light and combustion of its own commotion.

But when those ponies stand, finally quiet,
Their pure white manes and tails braided
With lilac and rock rose, the boys asleep

On their backs, when they stand,
Fragrant and shimmering, their forelocks
Damp with sweet oil, serene and silent
In the motionless dark of the deep
Riverside forest, then everyone can
Easily see and understand the magnificent
Silhouette, the restrained power, the adorned,
Unblemished and abiding beauty
That is the night.

Pattiann Rogers

Eggs. Dates and camel's milk.
Give this. In one hour the foal will
stand, in two will run. The care then of
women, the schooling from fear, clamor
of household, a prospect of saddles.

They kneel to it, folded
on its four perfect legs, stroke
the good back, the muscles bunched at the chest.
Its head, how the will shines large in it
as what may be used to overcome it.

The women of the horses comb out
their cruel histories of hair only for
the pleasure of horses, for the lost mares
on the Ridge of Yellow Horses, their white arms
praying the hair down breasts ordinary

as knees. The extent of their power,
this intimation of sexual wealth. From dread
in the eyes of horses are taken their songs.
In the white forests the last free horses
eat branches and roots, are hunted like deer
and carry no one.

A wedge of light where the doorway opens
the room—in it, a sickness of sleep.
The arms of the women, their coarse
white hair. In a bank of sunlight, a man
whitewashes the house he owns—no shores, no
worlds above it and farther, shrill, obsidian,
the high feasting of the horses.

Tess Gallagher

Horses and Men in Rain

Let us sit by the hissing steam radiator a winter's day, gray wind
    pattering frozen raindrops on the window,
And let us talk about milk wagon drivers and grocery delivery boys.

Let us keep our feet in wool slippers and mix hot punches—and talk
    about mail carriers and messenger boys slipping along the icy
    sidewalks.
Let us write of olden, golden days and hunters of the Holy Grail and
    men called "knights" riding horses in the rain, in the cold frozen
    rain for ladies they loved.

A roustabout hunched on a coal wagon goes by, icicles drip on his hat
    rim, sheets of ice wrapping the hunks of coal, the caravanserai a
    gray blur in slant of rain.
Let us nudge the steam radiator with our wool slippers and write
    poems of Launcelot, the hero, and Roland, the hero, and all the olden
    golden men who rode horses in the rain.

Carl Sandburg

II. HERE, NOW

. . . the casual shift

of her supple spine, her dignified shimmy.

—William Hathaway, "Bareback"

we struggled, the mare and I,
far beyond the Rubicon
through a mortal pit of night,
my arm in deeper than the stallion,
fingers straining toward petaled baby hooves
buried in pulsing crimson darkness,
teasing tangled parts around,
turning, sorting, re-arranging limbs—
pulling like hell when the time was right,
she pushing and grunting for life itself

and then, in a glorious rush of slop
he was out—new long-legged life
wrapped in wet blue film,
drawing first breath,
long lashes flicking,
nostrils flaring in the wide new world.

when he was clean and dry,
placenta out and safe from the dogs—
when he had, with a little help, stood and nursed
and lay back down to nap—
I sat on the stall floor, back against a bale,
an arm limp as spaghetti
across his velvet haunch,
sweat and effluvia drying in my hair
while the lady surveyed us both
with sweet alfalfa breath.

deep in weary bone
a flame of joy was leaping;
outside, snowflakes drifted through the dawn.

Michael List

Whoever knows the flowering leas
And the herd swept in its courses,
Running on, maws to the breeze:
Young horses! Ah, young horses!

Over ditches, grass, and stubble,
And along the hawthorn hedges
Wafts the string in nervous canter,
Sorrel, bay, white steed, and dapple!

Young summer mornings went away
In whiteness, and they neighed.
Cloud-hurled lightning sent them flying,
Full of fear they gallop shying.

Scenting through grey nostrils, rarely
They approach with nods and prances.
Starry pupils tremble warily
In the chinks of human glances.

Paul Boldt
Translated by Ernest Bernhardt-Kabisch

That mare stood in the field—
A big pine tree and a shed,
But she stayed in the open
Ass to the wind, splash wet.
I tried to catch her April
For a bareback ride,
She kicked and bolted
Later grazing fresh shoots
In the shade of the down
Eucalyptus on the hill.

Gary Snyder

Glutted, half asleep, browsing in
timothy grown so tall I see them
as though a pale-green stage scrim

they circle, nose to rump,
a trio of trained elephants.
It begins to rain, as promised.

Bit by bit they soak up drops
like laundry dampened to be ironed.
Runnels bedeck them. Their sides

drip like the ribs of very broad
umbrellas. And still they graze
and grazing, one by one let down

their immense, indolent penises
to drench the everlasting grass
with the rich nitrogen

that repeats them.

Maxine Kumin

1.

You have to turn your back to the animals.
   In theory it's better for them than shoes.
You have to hold them one leg at a time
   pinched with your legs to pick clean beneath each
hoof the sawdust, straw, mud-pack, pebbles, dung.
   The old ones stand patient, while the young may
stomp the hard barn floor to tell you to quit,
   or nod their long necks or quiver or huff.

2.

Rain has turned them skittish, the rain-flung leaves,
   whatever flies or crawls from a cold tree.
The scrape of your moon-crescent blade, as you
   carve each hoof hard as plastic or soft wood
down to the white heart, makes them want to grow
   wings, makes them want to fly or die or run.
You have to talk them down. Easy, you say
   in your own wind, soothing, easy now, whoa.

3.

But it's the long, continuous sighing
   breath of the file that stills them, for they know
you are through. You round the last edges down
   and smooth the hard breaks, as one by one they trot
through the tack-room door, muscle, mane, shadow,
   turning their backs to you. Now the sun is out.
Barn swallows brighten the loft. You watch them
   break into flight, hoofprints trickling with rain.

David Baker

When afternoon begins dissolving,
I take Spud and Snook to pasture,
each on a lead, with me between,
both roiling energy, to burst
at the gate and pound up the field
with flanks hard and eyes high,
daring any challenge to their fleet
dominion of that grassy world.

But there is a moment before the gate
where our way narrows between
rank cedars and dogwood by the lane,
when their nimble urgency not to be last
through that tapering speeds them,
and I must keep my feet safe
from theirs, my elbows high,

so as they surge
the crowding will lift and carry me—
so three rib cages crush and drive
in one flow, three backs weld
to rock as one, and I become part
of the deep charge against all fettering,
of shoulders churning like boulders
in a flood to deliver us

hoof-drumming ancient plains
with sun and new stems waving
belly high, so we can keep
with distance this heart safe
from what would creep against
our swifting over the globe—

all of this in a few strides
before the cedars are behind,
Spud and Snook ballet wider,

and with feet on the ground now
at the gate, I loosen their leads
and we stream apart

to know again the separate sky,
the close clothing of breeze,
to feel again so sharp the green
and beckoning of grass.

C. E. Greer

Here is a gift of Grace, not just from height
or your proud back—straight for a change,
but, oddly, in this spread-leg vulnerability.

Mostly you admire this miraculous horse,
are honored by the casual shift
of her supple spine, her dignified shimmy.

With the slow sureness of dream
her hooves crush a mixture of spices
from the hazy field swaying

in sunlight. Where quail, meadowlarks
whir up a fanfare for this stately progress
and your heart cannot quell

its beneficence to those wee squeals
of mice, so far below you. Truly
in this sublime posting between clouds

and pastureland, bowing only to the oak
limb, you know again that freedom,
freedom pedestrian equality took away.

Your thighs, her gleaming flanks
are fused in a current of pain,
for could there be joy in this rhythm,

sweet union of sinew and flesh, without ache?
No, you remember a warm throb
from the fly's cruel bite and you crave,

curiously, the bitterness of your mingled sweat.

William Hathaway

If he had stayed
in the four white walls
or alone in his patch, the untidy hedge
strewing its roses through empty hours
he would never have met the dark mare
whose neck he licked by the elderflower
whose kick snapped his straight cannonbone.

For sixteen weeks he must stand in the straw
watching the light wash and ebb.
All warmth will have flowed past when he stumbles out
November's wind raw on his leg.
Was it worth it? He shuffles, he cranes to the lane,
calls her, and calls her again.

Alison Brackenbury

Terrible

        a horse at night

   standing hitched alone

           in the still street

     and whinnying

          as if some sad nude astride him

had gripped hot legs on him

       and sung

           a sweet high hungry

      single syllable

               Lawrence Ferlinghetti

Darkness has feathered all night
downward into drifts. Vague bits of
dream. Discarded socks and shirt.
My feet sink in and track it
outside, where what's near
still recedes—woodpile, corral, the bay
mare's heavy head nodding
between the rails—I'm not
ready to open my other eyes.
The hungry horses loom like ships,
restless and dark against the sky.
One pokes a blunt nose out of the night,
into my hand, and a dream I had before waking
takes shape again—a familiar child,
my brother's new daughter left to my care
like the life-size doll I was given
one birthday, a time I was really part horse.
She was too expensive to be taken from her box.
"When you're older," they promised. Nearly
forty now, I kept forgetting to carry crackers
and milk to the hidden room where this child
drifted in her crib. Little by little she stopped
inventing words. Her warm cheeks
cooled to wax. I never even thought
to pick her up, my arms weren't real
as they weren't in the days when I
flourished my silk scarf for a tail.
When I munched what I was fed. When I tossed
my head and slept hard. Daylight
abruptly has flooded this yard.
My neglect, my night track, does not
burn off, but the horses turn to me
anyway, the bringer of buckets and hay.
All night they held some shape
of me in their heads like a dream—
a snip of red, perhaps, a weightless thing

drifting in and out of their view.
Now they dip their heads in the circle
of my arms. Their jaws closing over
the charged and magical grains are engines
churning up steam that would startle
their vast bodies away, even now,
if I raised a hand to them suddenly.

Leslie Ullman

I.

One after another, down the cement alley
under high dangling bulbs ablaze with halo
but faint light, I threw open their stall screens.
In the darkness I could hear their stamps
and soft splutters as they awoke from green
dreams. At my whistle the sudden rumble
arose, confused crashes from that scramble
shaking the great tin sheets. Cocked
tails flickered up from massive buttocks
into those long faces whose wild nodding
made eyes gleam white arcs for the thunder.

They must have seen a small shadow,
so squat and black in a vast square
of silver heaven as they snorted and chortled
out to me, pushing the smell of horse ahead
of them. And steaming and wheezing on
the frozen yard they rubbed their fat, rough
tongues on my head, jostled me to snow-
banks, nosed me everywhere for fruit
and sugar. Untucked and undone, sprawled on
ice, I was helpless with laughter, too weak
for breath, under their moist, quivering nostrils.

Merry eyes: I was drunk off the whiff of their
sweat, on the rhythmic turmoil of muscle
and hoof. Bright light in the morning.

William Hathaway

Amanda Dreams She Has Died and Gone to the Elysian Fields

This morning Amanda
lies down during breakfast.
The hay is hip high.
The sun sleeps on her back
as it did on the spine
of the dinosaur
the fossil bat
the first fish with feet
she was once.
A breeze fans
the deerflies from lighting.
Only a gaggle of gnats
housekeeps in her ears.
A hay plume sticks out of her mouth.

I come calling with a carrot
from which I have taken
the first bite.
She startles
she considers rising
but retracts the pistons
of her legs and accepts
as loose-lipped as a camel.

We sit together.
In this time and place
we are heart and bone.
For an hour
we are incorruptible.

Maxine Kumin

Just days after the vet came,
after the steroids that took
the fire out of the festering
sores—out of the flesh that in
the heat took the stings too
seriously and swelled into great
welts, wore thin and wept, calling
more loudly out to the green-
headed flies—I bathe you
and see your coat returning,
your deep force surfacing in a
new layer of hide: black wax
alive against weather and flies.

But this morning, misshapen
still, you look like an effigy,
something rudely made, something
made to be buffeted, or like
an old comforter—are they both
one in the end? So both a child

and a mother, with my sponge and
my bucket, I come to anoint, to
anneal the still weeping, to croon
to you *baby poor baby* for the sake
of the song, to polish you up,
for the sake of the touch, to a shine.
As I soothe you I surprise wounds
of my own this long time unmothered.
As you stand, scathed and scabbed,
with your head up, I swab. As you
press, I lean into my own loving
touch, for which no wound
is too ugly.

Linda McCarriston

Through early April cold,
these thin gray horses
have come near the house
as to a fence, and lean there
hungry for summer,
nodding their heads
with a nickering of twigs.

Their long legs are dusty
from standing for months
in winter's stall, and their eyes
are like a cloudy sky
seen through bare branches.

They are waiting for May
to come up from the barn
with her overalls pockets
stuffed with the fodder
of green. In a month
they will be slow and heavy,
their little snorts so sweet
you'll want to stand
among them, breathing.

Ted Kooser

The eye can hardly pick them out
From the cold shade they shelter in,
Till wind distresses tail and mane;
Then one crops grass, and moves about
—The other seeming to look on—
And stands anonymous again.

Yet fifteen years ago, perhaps
Two dozen distances sufficed
To fable them: faint afternoons
Of Cups and Stakes and Handicaps,
Whereby their names were artificed
To inlay faded, classic Junes—

Silks at the start: against the sky
Numbers and parasols: outside,
Squadrons of empty cars, and heat,
And littered grass: then the long cry
Hanging unhushed till it subside
To stop-press columns on the street.

Do memories plague their ears like flies?
They shake their heads. Dusk brims the shadows.
Summer by summer all stole away,
The starting-gates, the crowds and cries—
All but the unmolesting meadows.
Almanacked, their names live; they

Have slipped their names, and stand at ease,
Or gallop for what must be joy,
And not a fieldglass sees them home,
Or curious stop-watch prophesies:
Only the groom, and the groom's boy,
With bridles in the evening come.

Philip Larkin

Amanda, you'll be going
to Alpo or to Gaines
when you run out of luck;
the flesh flensed from your bones
your mammoth rib cage rowing
away to the renderer's
a dry canoe on a truck

while I foresee my corpse
slid feet first into fire
light as the baker's loaf
to make of me at least
a pint of potash spoor.
I'm something to sweeten the crops
when the clock hand stops.

Amanda, us in the woods
miles from home, the ground
upending in yellow flutes
that open but make no sound.
Ferns in the mouth of the brute,
chanterelles in the woman's sack . . .
what do I want for myself
dead center, bareback
on the intricate harp of your spine?
All that I name as mine

with the sure slow oxen of words:
feed sacks as grainy as boards
that air in the sun. A boy
who is wearing my mother's eyes.
Garlic to crush in the pan.
The family gathering in.
Already in the marsh
the yearling maples bleed
a rich onrush. Time slips
another abacus bead.

Let it not stick in the throat
or rattle a pane in the mind.
May I leave no notes behind
wishful, banal or occult
and you, small thinker in
the immensity of your frame,
may you be caught and crammed
midmouthful of the best grain
when the slaughterer's bullet slams
sidelong into your brain.

Maxine Kumin

When the plowblade struck
An old stump hiding under
The soil like a beggar's
Rotten tooth, they swarmed up
& Mister Jackson left the plow
Wedged like a whaler's harpoon.
The horse was midnight
Against dusk, tethered to somebody's
Pocketwatch. He shivered, but not
The way women shook their heads
Before mirrors at the five
& dime—a deeper connection
To the low field's evening star.
He stood there, in tracechains,
Lathered in froth, just
Stopped by a great, goofy
Calmness. He whinnied
Once, & then the whole
Beautiful, blue-black sky
Fell on his back.

Yusef Komunyakaa

All winter your brute shoulders strained against collars, padding
and steerhide over the ash hames, to haul
sledges of cordwood for drying through spring and summer,
for the Glenwood stove next winter, and for the simmering range.

In April you pulled cartloads of manure to spread on the fields,
dark manure of Holsteins, and knobs of your own clustered with oats.
All summer you mowed the grass in meadow and hayfield, the
    mowing machine
clacketing beside you, while the sun walked high in the morning;

and after noon's heat, you pulled a clawed rake through the same acres,
gathering stacks, and dragged the wagon from stack to stack,
and the built hayrack back, up hill to the chaffy barn,
three loads of hay a day from standing grass in the morning.

Sundays you trotted the two miles to church with the light load
of a leather quartertop buggy, and grazed in the sound of hymns.
Generation on generation, your neck rubbed the windowsill
of the stall, smoothing the wood as the sea smooths glass.

When you were old and lame, when your shoulders hurt bending
    to graze,
one October the man who fed you and kept you, and harnessed you
    every morning,
led you through corn stubble to sandy ground above Eagle Pond,
and dug a hole beside you where you stood shuddering in your skin,

and lay the shotgun's muzzle on the boneless hollow behind your ear,
and fired the slug into your brain, and felled you into your grave,
shoveling sand to cover you, setting goldenrod upright above you,
where by next summer a dent in the ground made your monument.

For a hundred and fifty years, in the pasture of dead horses,
roots of pine trees pushed through the pale curves of your ribs,
yellow blossoms flourished above you in autumn, and in winter
frost heaved your bones in the ground—old toilers, soil makers:

O Roger, Mackerel, Riley, Ned, Nellie, Chester, Lady Ghost.

Donald Hall

An Elegy on the Death of Dobbin, the Butterwoman's Horse

The death of faithful Dobbin I deplore;
Dame Jolt's brown horse, old Dobbin, is no more.
The cruel Fates have snapped his vital thread,
And Gammer Jolt bewails old Dobbin dead.
From stony Cudham down to watery Cray,
This honest horse brought butter every day,
Fresh butter meet to mix with nicest rolls,
And sometimes eggs, and sometimes geese and fowls;
And though this horse to stand had ne'er a leg,
He never dropped a goose, or broke an egg.
    Ye maids of Cray your buttered rolls deplore,
    Dame Jolt's brown horse, old Dobbin, is no more.

Oft did the squire, that keeps the great hall-house,
Invite the willing vicar to a goose;
For goose could make his kindred Muse aspire
From earth to air, from water to the fire;
    But now, alas! His towering spirit's fled,
    His Muse is foundered, for poor Dobbin's dead.
Last Friday was a luckless day, I wot,
For Friday last lean Dobbin went to pot;
No drinks could cherish, no prescriptions save;
In C——n's hounds he found a living grave:
    Weep all, and all (except sad dogs) deplore,
    Dame Jolt's brown horse, old Dobbin, is no more.

Skulk, Reynard, skulk in the securest grounds,
Now Dobbin hunts thee in the shape of hounds.
Late sure but slow he marched as foot could fall,
Sure to march slow whene'er he marched at all;
Now fleeter than the pinions of the wind,
He leaves the huntsman and the hunt behind,
Pursues thee o'er the hills and down the steep,
Through the rough copse, wide woods and waters deep,
Along th' unbounded plain, along the lea,
But has no pullet and no goose for thee.

Ye dogs, ye foxes, howl for Dobbin dead,
Nor thou, O Muse, disdain the tear to shed;
Ye maids of Cray your buttered rolls deplore,
Dame Jolt's brown horse, old Dobbin, is no more.

Francis Fawkes

One was a bay cowhorse from Piedra & the other was a washed out
    palomino
And both stood at the rail of the corral & both went on aging
In each effortless tail swish, the flies rising, then congregating again

Around their eyes & muzzles & withers.

Their front teeth were by now as yellow as antique piano keys &
    slanted to the angle
Of shingles on the maze of sheds & barn around them; their puckered

Chins were round & black as frostbitten oranges hanging unpicked
    from the limbs
Of trees all through winter like a comment of winter itself on
    everything
That led to it & found gradually the way out again.

In the slowness of time. Black time to white, & rind to blossom.
Deity is in the details & we are details among other details &
    we long to be

Teased out of ourselves. And become all of them.

The bay had worms once & had acquired the habit of drinking
    orange soda
From an uptilted bottle & nibbling cookies from the flat of a hand, &
    liked to do
Nothing else now, & the palomino liked to do nothing but gaze off

At traffic going past on the road beyond vineyards & it would follow
    each car
With a slight turning of its neck, back & forth, as if it were a thing

Of great interest to him.

If I rode them, the palomino would stumble & wheeze when it broke
Into a trot & would relapse into a walk after a second or two & then stop
Completely & without cause; the bay would keep going though it
    creaked

Underneath me like a rocking chair of dry, frail wood, & when I
    knew it could no longer

Continue but did so anyway, or when the palomino would stop &
    then take

Only a step or two when I nudged it forward again, I would slip off
    either one of them,
Riding bareback, & walk them slowly back, letting them pause when
    they wanted to.

At dawn in winter sometimes there would be a pane of black ice
    covering
The surface of the water trough & they would nudge it with their
    noses or muzzles,
And stare at it as if they were capable of wonder or bewilderment.

They were worthless. They were the motionless dusk & the
    motionless

Moonlight, & in the moonlight they were other worlds. Worlds
    uninhabited
And without visitors. Worlds that would cock an ear a moment
When the migrant workers come back at night to the sheds they were
    housed in

And turn a radio on, but only for a moment before going back to
    whatever

Wordless & tuneless preoccupation involved them.

The palomino was called Misfit & the bay was named Querido
    Flacco,
And the names of some of the other shapes had been Rockabye
And Ojo Pendejo & Cue Ball & Back Door Peter & Frenchfry &
    Sandman

And Rolling Ghost & Anastasia.

Death would come for both of them with its bridle of clear water
    in hand
And they would not look up from grazing on some patch of dry grass
    or even

Acknowledge it much; & for a while I began to think that the world

Rested on a limitless ossuary of horses where their bones & skulls
    stretched
And fused until only the skeleton of one enormous horse underlay
The smoke of cities & the cold branches of trees & and the distant

Whine of traffic on the interstate.

If I & by implication therefore anyone looked at them long enough
    at dusk
Or in moonlight he would know the idea of heaven & of life
    everlasting
Was so much blown straw or momentary confetti

At the unhappy wedding of a sister.

Heaven was neither the light nor was it the air, & if it took a
    physical form
It was splintered lumber no one could build anything with.

Heaven was a weight behind the eyes & one would have to stare
    right through it
Until he saw the air itself, just air, the clarity that took the shackles
    from his eyes
And the taste of the bit from his mouth & knocked the rider off
    his back

So he could walk for once in his life.

Or just stand there for a moment before he became something else,
    some
Flyspeck on the wall of a passing & uninterruptible history whose
    sounds claimed
To be a cheering from bleachers but were actually no more than the
    noise

Of cars entering the mouths of a tunnel.

And in the years that followed he would watch them in the
    backstretch or the far turn
At Santa Anita or Del Mar. Watch the way they made it all seem
    effortless,

Watch the way they were explosive & untiring.

And then watch the sun fail him again & slip from the world,
   & watch
The stands slowly empty. As if all moments came back to this one,
   inexplicably
To this one out of all he might have chosen—Heaven with ashes
   in its hair

And filling what were once its eyes—this one with its torn tickets
Littering the aisles & the soft racket the wind made. This one.
   Which was his.

And if the voice of a broken king were to come in the dusk &
   whisper
To the world, that grandstand with its thousands of empty seats,

Who among the numberless you have become desires this moment

Which comprehends nothing more than loss & fragility &
   the fleeing of flesh?
He would have to look up at the quickening dark & say: *Me. I do.
   It's mine.*

Larry Levis

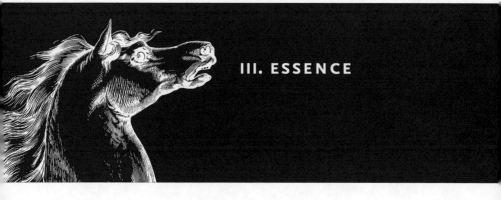

III. ESSENCE

They do not wish that they were otherwhere.

—Gwendolyn Brooks, "Horses Graze"

Cows graze.
Horses graze.
They
eat
eat
eat.
Their graceful heads
are bowed
bowed
bowed
in majestic oblivion.
They are nobly oblivious
to your follies,
your inflation,
the knocks and nettles of administration.
They
eat
eat
eat.
And at the crest of their brute satisfaction,
with wonderful gentleness, in affirmation,
they lift their clean calm eyes and they lie down
and love the world.
They speak with their companions.
They do not wish that they were otherwise.
Perhaps they know that creature feet may press
only a few earth inches at a time,
that earth is anywhere earth,
that an eye may see,
wherever it may be,
the Immediate arc, alone, of life, of love.

                              Gwendolyn Brooks

Just off the highway to Rochester, Minnesota,
Twilight bounds softly forth on the grass.
And the eyes of those two Indian ponies
Darken with kindness.
They have come gladly out of the willows
To welcome my friend and me.
We step over the barbed wire into the pasture
Where they have been grazing all day, alone.
They ripple tensely, they can hardly contain their happiness
That we have come.
They bow shyly as wet swans. They love each other.
There is no loneliness like theirs.
At home once more,
They begin munching the young tufts of spring in the darkness.
I would like to hold the slenderer one in my arms,
For she has walked over to me
And nuzzled my left hand.
She is black and white,
Her mane falls wild on her forehead,
And the light breeze moves me to caress her long ear
That is delicate as the skin over a girl's wrist.
Suddenly I realize
That if I stepped out of my body I would break
Into blossom.

James Wright

Walking at night, blood and bone
coaxing flesh down a country path,
I come across the fenced-in sorrel
grazing in a light-green field
so lit by the moon it glows
like wheat, and stop to call her name.

But I have nothing to give, no
sweet thing except my hand in her mane,
my voice in her ear. Even as clouds
drag their long darkness over the
field I call and wait, wanting to feel
her living skull, her warm breath blowing,

nose nudging my hand for more, still more.

Roger Pfingston

For a moment there is no bit, no whip, no wagon,
no heavy load—only another's neck
to lean your head on.
Infinity of bliss.
Under the skin tenderness rolls with deep waves,
and breath flows into velvet nostrils,
and night like a black star falls into manes.
The humans sleep.
Meanwhile the horses drink
bliss—muzzle by muzzle—from misty rivers,
from a moon melted in cups of dew,
from half-closed eyes—the horses
drink bliss like jet-black rainbows—solemn and mute,

until the whip of dawn lashes a bloody streak
across night's gentle flank.

Vizma Belševica
Translated by Ilze Klavina Mueller

Way down the field, where the ground
was humped as the back of a dragon
and none of us ever went,

the horses stopped grazing and lifted
their heads. It was a Maine
summer, the midday heat

coming upon us like a sneeze,
a violent, brief strength under
which the horses ranged,

gliding over the green in a knot
of bronze. I'd grow drowsy
watching them

drift like bees
silent, intent, woven
into the landscape

in a way
I thought I could never be, my
absurd awareness of *self*

the hole in the whole.
I remember the alien peace I felt,
once, when I tried to embrace

the colt, his swollen barrel
of a stomach too huge to get
my arm around, but even so we communed

that way for a few
seconds, and, for those few seconds,
I belonged to the scene, I was unbroken.

At the end of the day,
when I fed them meal and hay
from the barn, there was a protocol

the horses followed:
to each his own
dish, and all ate

with abandon, staring blindly
as they champed. Later, they might
move toward the trough

at the side of the barn,
but I rarely saw them drink
from it, as though drinking were a private devotion

not to be witnessed.
When I think of that trough,
I think of the day

I found a kitten
sealed like a fly in amber
in its depth. The barn cats

had hardly looked pregnant,
and then there were two kittens,
and then there were two deaths,

the first one
kicked, and the second
drowned. Seamlessly found,

seamlessly lost. The barn cats
frisked the back field, unfazed.
I buried the kitten with a stiff

efficiency. Night sank.
The horses bowed their heads
to drink.

Jean Monahan

Too soon, too soon, a man will come
To lock the gate, and drive them home.
Then, neighing softly through the night,
The mare will nurse her shoulder bite.
Now, lightly fair, through lock and mane
She gazes over the dusk again,
And sees her darkening stallion leap
In grass for apples, half asleep.

Lightly, lightly, on slender knees
He turns, lost in a dream of trees.
Apples are slow to find this day,
Someone has stolen the best away.
Still, some remain before the snow,
A few, trembling on boughs so low
A horse can reach them, small and sweet:
And some are tumbling to her feet.

Too soon, a man will scatter them,
Although I do not know his name,
His age, or how he came to own
A horse, an apple tree, a stone.
I let those horses in to steal
On principle, because I feel
Like half a horse myself, although
Too soon, too soon, already. Now.

James Wright

All day we followed the tracks of the wild horses
On foot, taking turns at resting,
Eating our cold food as we walked each way
They turned to escape us. They disappeared
Sometimes behind rough-shouldered ridges, up canyons,
But we hurried after them and found them
Too soon for grazing. They swam rivers
That might have made them safe from wolves
But not from *our* hunger: it was behind our eyes
And not in our mouths. As we came nearer, nearer,
Their heads would turn to us, then turn
Away, they would go away aimlessly,
Hating our smell as we loved theirs and hating
The sight of us as we loved theirs, the headstrong
Round-rumped tangle-maned light-footed
Windy-tailed horses who would belong to us.

Already, others of our slow kind were flying
Above four hooves, their feet leaving the earth
Like birds flying as far as we could go
In five of our old sleeps. Now following after
At evening, we gave them no rest, gave nothing
But hunger and that other emptiness:
Fear of our strangeness. Some of us slept by water
While they stood in the distance, darkening,
Smelling it with dry nostrils, waiting to drink
As deep as the coming night but seeing us waiting
There for something they must have known was their hearts
And their whole lives to come.

In the morning, they were kneeling, lying down, rising
And trotting again, then slowing, walking no faster
Than we kept walking after them. They stumbled
And fell once more and stayed where they were
As if dying, their white-flecked mouths
And white-cornered eyes all turning
As we touched them on their trembling withers to tell them
What they were, what they would learn from us.

David Wagoner

The Judas-Horse

I.

This one wild enough to tame with enough
time, whose brown mane flicks to flame, and this one
roughed-up in the weather, winded, ruffled
and muscled, running like wind, hooves churning,
and two more, then three charging, galloping
over the blasted prairie hilltop grass—
burr-coated, mud-matted, nicked by hooves
in battle or mating's warrior moments.

2.

The thighs tighten—a canter in the ring.
The toe tips out to turn. Your hands above
the withers hold the reins, "as glass,"
lest the horse find meaning in a jostle . . .
The usual mode of taking the wild
horses, is, by throwing the *laso*, whilst
pursuing them at full speed, and dropping
a noose over their necks—so Catlin writes—

3.

thus, they are "choked down," until the horse falls
from want of breath, and lies helpless on the ground,
where it soon becomes docile and conquered.
Or "creasing." This is done by shooting them
through the gristle on the top of the neck,
which stuns them so they fall, and are secured
with the hobbles on their feet; after which
they rise again without fatal injury.

4.

I have loved you wild enough to hurt you.
I know this now. I have been docile, conquered,
dependent. The smallest movements matter.
Catlin paints the Mandan buffalo-men
—1832, upper Missouri—
flying, a few paces from the herd,
atop horses only lightly tamed by
a hand on the animal's nose, over

5.

its eyes, at length "to breathe in its nostrils."
Our love is furious and calm. Thus we
ride over the sweet-smelling earth neither
toward each other nor away. The horse, he writes,
yields gladly—. This one a flurry of dust.
This one nose down, tail flung, flying like foaming
water. And this one, the tame one, running
with the others, to lead them through the gate.

David Baker

The Bronco That Would Not Be Broken

A little colt—bronco, loaned to the farm
To be broken in time without fury or harm,
Yet black crows flew past you, shouting alarm,
Calling "Beware," with lugubrious singing . . .
The butterflies there in the bush were romancing,
The smell of the grass caught your soul in a trance,
So why be afearing the spurs and the traces,
O bronco that would not be broken of dancing?

You were born with the pride of the lords great and olden
Who danced, through the ages, in corridors golden.
In all the wide farm place the person most human.
You spoke out so plainly with squealing and capering,
With whinnying, snorting, contorting and prancing,
As you dodged your pursuers, looking askance,
With Greek-footed figures, and Parthenon paces,
O bronco that would not be broken of dancing.

The grasshoppers cheered. "Keep whirling," they said.
The insolent sparrows called from the shed
"If men will not laugh, make them wish they were dead."
But arch were your thoughts, all malice displacing,
Though the horse killers came, with snake whips advancing.
You bantered and cantered away your last chance.
And they scourged you, with hell in their speech and their faces,
O bronco that would not be broken of dancing.

"Nobody cares for you," rattled the crows,
As you dragged the whole reaper, next day, down the rows.
The three mules held back, yet you danced on your toes.
You pulled like a racer, and kept the mules chasing.
You tangled the harness with bright eyes side-glancing,
While the drunk driver bled you—a pole for a lance—
And the giant mules bit at you—keeping their places,
O bronco that would not be broken of dancing.

In that last afternoon your boyish heart broke.
The hot wind came down like a sledge-hammer stroke.
The bloodsucking flies to a rare feast awoke.
And they searched out your wounds, your death warrant tracing.
And the merciful men, their religion enhancing,
Stopped the red reaper, to give you a chance.
Then you died on the prairie, and scorned all disgraces,
O bronco that would not be broken of dancing.

Vachel Lindsay

The Appaloosa

The one horse you gave me
you took back when she went insane,
when she began to chew wood
instead of the expensive grain
we bought from the feed store,
the grain that had the sweet smell
of molasses and was good for even
us to chew. She turned into
an ugly thing with her wild thoughts,
and I forgot about the beauty
expected of her when her blanket
filled out and complemented
her chestnut body and the name
the Nez Percé gave her. She rotted
and began to stink of promises
gone wrong, of gods avenging
their defilement. A man who knew
what to do with useless horses
came and took her away in
a wooden trailer she tried to chew,
and my tears welled up in huge drops
before they splattered on the ground,
as I trembled and realized I would have
to give up her own ghost for her,
ghost which she did not have, ghost
which she came here beautifully without.

Michael S. Weaver

choosing the gelding, younger, more placid,
I remember my mother chose my brother

over me for that reason, today I am
packing my bad girl off to auction,

the whites of her eyes, red, the vet's
hypnotic voice, *temper*, he says, *such*

a temper, but her loveliness outweighs
everything, the shape of her head,

the neck arch, I think of Isak Dinesen
leaving Africa—"these horses!" she cried

in goodbye—my first mare the one I should
have had as a girl when I was bolder,

one day vicious, indomitable, the next
crying at the gate, already I've forgotten

she bit me with fury, with her hind legs
struck me down, that day I took a crop,

beat her until I could no longer raise
my arm, the look in that mare's eyes said

it made no difference, there was no way to
make this bad girl good, when she struck me

across the face, was that the look my mother
saw in me? lovely thing, the dreams I had

for her, I am shipping her off the way
my mother did me, her black tail flowing

in my dreams, now I wait for the van,
she waits—little clock—by the fence

haunches spread, the stallion watches her
tail cocked, tart, sweating from head to hoof

flesh hot as stove burners, selling this mare
what is it I send to auction?

Jana Harris

There's a window here
and outside a horse is eating.
Because it's winter
I can see the horse's breath,
although in here it's warm.
What thoughts are you having?
Do they rise like your breath?
Today I will ride you
and try to know.

Jason S. Greer

It was from a window I first saw the horses.

It was winter in Berlin: a light
with no light, a sky without sky.

The air white as a loaf of wet bread.

And there, by the window, bitten off
by the teeth of the winter, a deserted arena.

Then, all of a sudden, ten horses
led by a man, moved into the snow.

Their passing left hardly a ripple, like fire,
but they filled a whole universe
void to my eyes, until then. Ablaze
with perfection, they moved like ten gods, colossal
and grand in the hoof, with dreamy and elegant manes.

Their rumps were like planets or oranges.

Their color was honey and amber and fire.

Their necks were like pillars
carved in the stone of their arrogance,
and out of vehement eyes their energy
glared from within like a prisoner.

There, in the silence of midday
in a soiled and slovenly winter
the horses' intensity was rhythm
and blood, the importunate treasure of being.

I looked—looked till my whole force reawakened.
This was the innocent fountain, the dance in the gold,
the sky, the fire still alive in the beautiful.

I've forgotten the wintry gloom of Berlin.

I will never forget the light of the horses.

> *Pablo Neruda*
> *Translated by Ben Belitt*

The horses go down at dawn.

They enter the golden lake and move on—
wave against wave
of arched necks and manes—
into the dazzling light.
Naked boys
bathe their haunches
    and they raise
    their antique figures,
drunk with light.
They listen,
ears attentive,
to the delicate bugle of morning,
and see
the vast battlefield.
Then they dream—
    a remote boldness
    breaks through—
soaring back
to the heroic days
when swords
returned the sun's thrusts,
white stallions
squadrons of silver
and distant cries
of birds
and wind.

    But they return

      (Time
      is the whip)

With the lash
they file toward land,
heads bowed,
and yoked
    to the wagon
      the dream

remains
    behind;
      the wind's
        asleep.

Pablo Antonio Cuadra
Translated by Grace Schulman and Ann McCarthy de Zavala

And I've left at first light, birds in their nests,
on a short-haired stallion, sired wild, huge,
attacking, backing, banking, outflanking
all at once—a boulder
                barreled off the mountain on an avalanche.
Blood's hue simmers in his gray.
The saddle-felt sails
             straight off his back
like a pebble intercepted by a cataract.
He surges to second wind,
thunder under the sea-surge
                of his heartbeat,
like a kettle at full boil.
He flows, while the floating mares
falter and go stringhalt.
The light young jockey blows
                  right off his back;
he whips the clothes
             clean off the hard-eyed heavy rider.
He spins like a boy's toy
              hurler-twirler whirled on a string.

Thighs of a gazelle, cannons of an ostrich.
He trots like a wolf, runs like a young fox.
Deep in the heart-girth; the gap between his gaskins
filled to overflow,
and no bone below them askew.
Smooth across the spine as a bride's new griddlestone,
solid as a mill-slab in the ribs.
Blood of big game at his throatlatch—a stain
like tincture of henna combed into an old man's beard.

We sighted a herd, and the cows were like the white-robed
vestals walking circles round the altar-stone.
They turned,
they flew like beads from a breaking necklace,

necklace off a neck
whose father's and mother's

                           brothers sit high in the tribe.
We rode down on the fastest;
                    the rest
of the herd ran hard together, far in his dust.
And he leaped between lead bull and cow
without breaking a lather.

That day, in sum, there was meat on the fire—
some hung high to cure, some turned
at once to steak and stew.

Sunset breeze, and the eye seemed
almost insufficient to sustain
examination of him, looking him hoof to poll.
He stood saddled and bridled,
close in my gaze, the night through.

Imru' al-Qays
Translated by Suzanne P. Stetkevych

It must have been Lisa's voice
since Piano was waiting when we got there,
the bay doors barely open and her white
face running the bars along her stall.
Then Lisa brought her out into the hall
to brush her down in order to show
the wood sheen under the dust and how
the tension of the body, if she stood
still long enough, could make her look
like she was floating standing. And given
time, in the broken bird light falling
from the loft, she seemed to float,
nodding and letting her neck, a third
of all of her, bend to the floor,
where she swept, with little breaths,
each loose and useless piece until
she found the somewhere solid that
she wanted, striking the heavy air
to let us know, marking the place
to tell us, in a second, she could fly.
Her body had already started to shine,
but it was her blaze that gave her eyes
their depth against the touch and Lisa's soft talk.
And it was the eyes that sometimes flared
against the words. Lisa said she was wild
because she was young. And bored, too,
when she couldn't get out, yet never bored
the way some horses dance from side to side,
spelling their weight, pressing their radiant,
stalled foreheads into the walls, or the way
some horses disappear inside, having
drawn and redrawn circles. The barn was
full of the noise and silences of horses.
And filled with Lisa's voice in counter-
point: and Lisa's horse's stillnesses—
like love or what love's moment's stillness
really is, hands-high, and restless.

Stanley Plumly   67

We have chosen our days among creatures
of bone memory from eons of the herd

keeping strength and fear and trust
in hard limb and large eye,

with no famous place, no city—
only such fortune as brought us

to move with them through each arriving,
each leaving of light from the earth.

C. E. Greer

from "If Poetry Were Not a Morality"

       I knew her grandfather had to be
one of those chiefs who could never

get enough horses. Who if he had two hundred
wanted a hundred more and a hundred more
after that. Maybe he'd get up in the night and go
out among them, or watch their grazing
from a distance under moonlight. He'd pass his mind
over them where they pushed their muzzles into
each other's flanks and necks and their horseness
gleamed back at him like soundless music until
he knew something he couldn't know
as only himself, something not to be told again
even by writing down the doing

of it. I meet him like that sometimes,
wordless and perfect, with more horses than he
can ride or trade or even know why
he has.

                      Tess Gallagher

What can I dedicate to you, lord? Say
it, you who taught the beasts their perfect ear.
My memory at the end of a spring day,
its evening, Russia, seeing a horse appear. . . .

Across from the village a white horse came
alone, with a big rope hobbling its fore
fetlock. Alone all night. Night overcame
those meadows. How his shock of mane with rigor

pounded against his neck in rhythm with
his arrogance in his grossly shackled gal-
lop. How the springs of his stallion blood leapt!

The horse felt all those distances he swept
away! He sang and heard! Your round of myth
was sealed in him. His image I regale.

Rainer Maria Rilke
Translated by Willis Barnstone

Horse, you flame thrower,
you shark-mouthed man,
you laughter at the end of poems,
you brown furry locomotive
whipping the snow, I am
a pale shadow beside you.
Your nostrils open like field glasses
and can smell all my fear. I am
a silver spoon. You are a four-footed
wing. If I am thirsty you feed me
through an eyedropper, for you are a
gallon drum. Beside you I feel
like a little girl with a papa
who is screaming.

         And yet and yet,
field horse lapping the grass
like stars and then your droppings,
sweet melons, all brown and
good for gardens and carrots.
Your soft nose would nuzzle me
and my fear would go out singing
into its own body.

Anne Sexton

This time
it was only them
being let out
to the damp alfalfa
of landscapes
by Duncanson and Constable,
to celebrate their legs
after a late August shower
before evening's golden web
had disappeared in mist,
turned back
to thunderhead.

Still, amid
the pristine opinions
of crickets and dove,
the spray of rainbow
across the sky
and family venturing forth
to the porch
to choose cloud homes
and watch hydrangeas
lift their burdens
of blue clusters,

it was eerie
how they appeared
on the horizon
single file like a vein
of lightning,
nothing but verb
as they branched out
and circled the valley
trampling dandelion
and clover—
from mane to croup

to fetlock,
every ounce
brighter than stars.

The whole while
seemed so Morphean
the way they moved
in tandem, stirring
those fiery heads
from grazing
for every invisible noise,
and then like
a white tide,
moved for hidden shores
as if answering
some otherworldly call.

Philosophers remind
time and again
that the joys
of metaphor
are best applied
to such events,
to squarely challenge,
as Euripides did,
god and beast
and mystery to come.

But that evening
there wasn't a one of us
who didn't think
of Revelation
in a literal sense,
who didn't wonder
of the red, the black,
the pale horses
yet to come.

Across the distance
our ears imagined
the fugue of hooves
as the last of them
breached the mist
and left us to
a few remaining moments
of verdancy and rainbow,
as they vanished
with a fire
that promised
they'd be back
the first chance
they could.

                    Claude Wilkinson

IV. HARNESSED

Say this of horses: engines leave behind
  No glorious legacy of waving manes
—Minnie Hite Moody, "Say This of Horses"

Pale as the morning star
in the hour of sunrise

he advances proudly,
caparisoned with a saddle of gold.

One who saw him going with me
into battle, envied me and said:

"Who bridled Dawn with the Pleiades?
Who saddled lightning with the half moon?"

Umayyah Ibn Abi Salt
Translated by Cola Franzen

Across the ages they come thundering
   On faithful hoofs, the horses man disowns.
Their velvet eyes are wide with wondering;
   They whinny down the wind in silver tones
Vibrant with all the bugles of old wars;
   Their nostrils quiver with the summer scent
Of grasses in deep fields lit by pale stars
   Hung in a wide and silent firmament,
And in their hearts they keep the dreams of earth
   Their patient plodding furrowed to the sun
Unnumbered springs before the engine's birth
   Doomed them to sadness and oblivion.
Across the swift new day I watch them go,
   Driven by wheel and gear and dynamo.

Say this of horses: engines leave behind
   No glorious legacy of waving manes
And wild, proud hearts, and heels before the wind,
   No heritage of ancient Arab strains
Blazes within a cylinder's cold spark;
   An engine labors with a sullen force,
Hoarding no dreams of acres sweet and dark:

   No love for man has ever surged through wire.
Along the farthest slopes I hear the rumble
   Of these last hoofs—tomorrow they will be still;
Then shall the strength of countless horses crumble
   The staunchest rock and level the highest hill;
A man who made machines to gain an hour
   Shall lose himself before their ruthless power.

Minnie Hite Moody

Horse Description from "The Golden Ode"

And many a bitter morning of wind and cold
    I curbed
when its reins were in the hand
    of the north wind,

I defended the tribe, my battle gear borne
    by a winning courser,
her reins my sash when I
    went forth at dawn.

Then I mounted a lookout post
    on a narrow, wind-blown peak
whose dust rose to the banners
    of the foe

Until, when daylight dipped its hand into
    the all-concealing night
and darkness veiled the crotches of
    each mountain pass,

To the plain I descended, and my mare
    held erect her neck
like the date-palms stripped trunk at which
    the picker's courage fails.

I spurred her to a speed
    fit for the ostrich chase,
until, when she was heated through
    and her bones were nimble,

Her light leathern saddle slipped,
    sweat flowed from her neck,
and her saddle girth
    was soaked with froth.

She coursed, head held high and thrusting
    in the bridle, racing headlong
like a thirsting dove to water when
    her flock beats urgent wings.

Labid ibn Rabi`ah
Translated by Suzanne P. Stetkevych

Fast, fast, with heels and wild spurning,
The dark-grey charger fled:
He burst through ranks of fighting men;
He sprang o'er heaps of dead.
His bridle far out-streaming,
His flanks all blood and foam,
He sought the southern mountains,
The mountains of his home.
The pass was steep and rugged,
The wolves they howled and whined;
But he ran like a whirlwind up the pass,
And he left the wolves behind.
Through many a startled hamlet
Thundered his flying feet;
He rushed through the gate of Tusculum,
He rushed up the long white street;
He rushed by tower and temple,
And paused not from his race
Till he stood before his master's door
In the stately market-place.
And straightway round him gathered
A pale and trembling crowd,
And when they knew him, cries of rage
Brake forth, and wailing loud:
And women rent their tresses
For their great prince's fall;
And old men girt on their old swords,
And went to man the wall.
But, like a graven image,
Black Auster kept his place,
And ever wistfully he looked
Into his master's face.
The raven-mane that daily,
With pats and fond caresses,
The young Herminia washed and combed
And twined in even tresses,

And decked with coloured ribands
From her own gay attire,
Hung sadly o'er her father's corpse
In carnage and in mire.

Thomas Babington Macaulay

In the war where many men fell
Wind blew in a ring, and was grass.
Many horses fell also to rifles
On a track in the Philippine Islands
And divided their still, wiry meat
To be eaten by prisoners.
I sat at the finish line
At the end of the war

Knowing that I would live.
Long grass went around me, half wind,
Where I rode the rail of the infield
And the dead horses travelled in waves
On past the finishing post.
Dead wind lay down in live grass,
The flowers, pounding like hooves,
Stood up in the sun and were still,

And my mind, like a fence on fire,
Went around those unknown men:
Those who tore from the red, light bones
The intensified meat of hunger
And then lay down open-eyed
In a raw, straining dream of new life.
Joy entered the truth and flowed over
As the wind rose out of the grass

Leaping with red and white flowers:
Joy in the bone-strewn infield
Where clouds of barbed wire contained
Men who ran in a vision of greenness,
Sustained by the death of beasts,
On the tips of the sensitive grass blades,
Each footstep putting forth petals,
Their bones light and strong as the wind.

James Dickey

Its nostrils black, the horse plunges
Raging under its rider, under the age.
The age flashes by just as rambunctious,
but the rider—
can not jump off or dodge.

An arrow or a sharp spearhead will pierce
crunching into a stranger's breast.
In the next century someone will paint
the rider falling from his destry,

And the empty-saddled steed will bolt
through a field of thorns and sawgrass,
scenting blood and the turning-point of battle . . .
With his rider, a centaur—
          without, only a horse.

He will give a long whinny at the brink
and, raising to the constellations his skull,
Plunge down the cliff, still steaming,
without ever understanding the world.

Aleksandr Tkachenko
Translated by Maia Tekses

No night weeps blacker at the blackened grates
Than in the lightless shaft the sightless nag.
It thinks the meadow that it bitterly tastes
In every blade of hay will never come back.

Through the dead rock's black flesh it snuffs the scents
Of Death and looks at him with its dead eyes;
All night in his sole company it spends
And loathes the harnesses in which it plies.

The boy who drives it through the narrow galleries
Tries if some bread and sugar will cheer it up.
It can no longer laugh as horses laugh,
The black night stays and burrows in its eyes.

Only when, with the scent of sap and leaves,
Forest-fresh timber down the mine is thrust,
By sudden madness gripped, it heaves
Its bony head and stomps the boy into the dust.

The mountain's black night, in explosion flaring,
From its worn hooves strikes sparks like gold.
Ere distress signals sound their blaring,
The blind horse multiplies a hundredfold,

And crashes through the labyrinthine mass,
And, bolting, tumbles down the rocky flight
Of stairs, and whinnies through the prairie grass,
On which dead horses reign in deathless might.

Paul Zech
Translated by Ernest Bernhardt-Kabisch

Just one crack against the sandbar
and the grain freighter crumbled into
itself like paper in flames, all the lifeboats
and blankets, the tons of yeasty wheat
sucked down so fast the tumbling sailors

still carried in the flat backs of their brains
the sensations of the galley, smoky with mutton fat,
someone's hiccup, someone's red woolen sleeve
still dragging itself across their eyes

even as the long sleeve of the water closed over them.

It was 3 A.M., the third of November, 1891.
Just to the south of this chaos, where the Columbia
washes over the Pacific,

there was shouting, the groan of stable doors,
and over the beachfront, a dozen
horses were running. Trained
with a bucket of timothy to swim rescue,
they passed under the beam of the Klipsan lighthouse,
passed out from the grasses, alfalfa,
deep snores and the shuffle of hooves,

and entered the black ocean.
Just heads then, stretched nostrils and necks
swimming out to the sailors
who were themselves just heads, each brain
a sputtering flame above the water.
Delirious, bodies numb, they answered
the stallions with panic—
So this is the death parade, Neptune's
horses lashed up from Akasha!—
                              And still,

through some last act of the self, when
the tails floated past they grabbed on,

then watched as the horses
returned to themselves, as the haunches
pulled, left then right, and the small circles
of underhooves stroked up in unison. Here
was the sound of sharp breathing, troubled
with sea spray, like bellows left out in the rain,
and here the texture of sand on the belly,
on the shirt and thigh, on the foot
with its boot, and the naked foot—and then, finally,
the voices, the dozens gathered to
cheer the rescue, the long bones of the will,
causing hands to close over those rippling tails,
yellow teeth to close over the timothy.

Linda Bierds

If I could get Yeats on a horse, I'd put a new rhythm into English poetry.
—Ezra Pound

Get on, expecting the worst—a mount like a statue
Or a bucking runaway.
If neither happens, if this bay mare holds still,
Then you're off
The ground, not touching the ground except through her
Four stilted corners
Which now plop up and down as carefully
In the mud by the road
As if those hoofprints behind her were permanent.
You're in the saddle
As she clip-clops up the path on a slack rein,
Her nose leading the way
Under the pine boughs switching like her tail.
Give in. Sit still.
It won't be hard to let her have her head:
It's hers by a neck;
She'll keep it against your geeing, hawing, or whoaing.
This one's been bred
To walk from daybreak to darkness in the mountains
Up trail or down
And will do it without you tomorrow. The apparatus
Cinching and bridling her,
The leather and metal restraints for a prisoner
Who *won't* be convenient,
Who *won't* do what she's told or listen to reason,
Are mostly for show:
For example, take this place you're passing now—
Tall stumps and boulders,
Thirty degrees of slope and a narrow trail—
A time for judgment,
A time for the nice control of cause and effect.
Do you see the flies

Clustered around her eyelids, nipping their salt?
Or the humming wasp
Tossed from her tail to her rump where it sinks in?
Suddenly swivelling
And sliding, jerking tight as a slipknot
And rearing out from under
Arched like a cow and a half humped over the moon,
She leaves you alone,
And you part company on the only terms
Possible: hers being yours—
No straddler of winged horses, no budding centaur,
But a man biting the dust.

David Wagoner

The horse moves
independently
without reference
to his load

He has eyes
like a woman and
turns them
about, throws

back his ears
and is generally
conscious of
the world. Yet

he pulls when
he must and
pulls well, blowing
fog from

his nostrils
like fumes from
the twin
exhausts of a car.

William Carlos Williams

Beginning in half darkness,
The horses up for hours with the men,
The quick slush of riding hoofs comes easily
Sounding around the muddy track, distantly
Fading into nearness and out of it again.
The high hum of singing from the gangling grooms
Beats a morning blues harmony, modified for years
By the endless running hoofs.
In the green morning—with the light
Mist of dawn rolling with the horse's breath
And the drifting ground smoke of fires
Built for water- and hand-warming—
Moving under the young sun,
The horse with his quick slush comes sounding
Easily off the track, snorting at the groom's
Caressing, cool hand.
                         Easy, easy, baby boy—
He loves the dumb horse with the dumbness
Of his cool hands upon him, rubbing down
The hard-veined animal powered by slim,
Brainy legs, poised delicately under the heaving body,
Like mobiles of bones and tendon, wired beautifully,
Just this side of stillness and of death.

Edward Parone

The sky unfolding its blankets to free
The morning.
Chill on the air. Clean odor of stables.
The grandstand green as the turf,
The pavilion flaunting its brilliance
For no one.
Beyond hurdles and hedges, swans, circling, cast
A contemplative radiance over the willow's shadows.
Day pales the toteboard lights,
Gilds the balls, heightens the stripes of the poles.
Dirt shines. White glisten of rails.
The track is bright as brine.
Their motion a flowing,
From prick of the ear to thick tail's shimmering drift,
The horses file forth.
Pink nostrils quiver, as who know they are showing their colors.
Ankles lift, as who hear without listening.
The bay, the brown, the chestnut, the roan have loaned
Their grace to the riders who rise in the stirrups, or hunch
Over the withers, gentling with mumbled song.
A mare ambles past, liquid eye askance.
Three, then four, canter by: voluptuous power
Pours through their muscles,
Dancing in pulse and nerve.
They glide in the stretch as on skis.
Two
Are put to a drive:
Centaur energy bounding as the dirt shudders, flies
Under the wuthering pace,
Hushes the hooves' thunders,
The body's unsyllabled eloquence rapidly
Dying away.
Dark-skinned stable-boys, as proud as kin
Of their display of vivacity, elegance,
Walk the racers back.
Foam laces the girths, sweaty haunches glow.

Slowly returning from the track, the horse is
Animal paradigm of innocence, discipline, force.
Blanketed, they go in.
Odor of earth
Enriches azuring air.

Babette Deutsch

The constant cry against an old order,
An order constantly old,
Is itself old and stale.

Here is the world of a moment,
Fitted by men and horses
For hymns,

In a freshness of poetry by the sea,
In galloping hedges,
In thudding air:

Beyond any order,
Beyond any rebellion,
A brilliant air

On the flanks of horses,
On the clear grass,
On the shapes of the mind.

Wallace Stevens

All was dingy and dull in late afternoon.
We sat on wooden benches, silent and sweating,
Becalmed there beyond expectation,
Sated by blue-ribbon sheep and candy, waiting
On the dusty last day of the fair to see
The horse-pulling (whatever that might be).

So underplayed a scene in the exhausted air,
We almost fell asleep. Why had we come,
I mean on earth at all, not only here?
Loud-speakers blared out some lost child's name.
The horses sneezed and shuffled in the heat.
We were all waiting with lead in our feet.

And then the darkness lifted like a dream.
We were back in some old heroic place—
Three men led in the first competing team.
Horses? No, gods! An arrogance of grace,
A dancing lightness held in three dwarfs' hands,
They swept like music past the silent stands.

It was brute power contained in sweet decorum,
The noble heads held high as in a frieze.
Relaxed and gay, they made the dust a forum.
It took us like a shout, tears in our eyes,
As they pranced up so lightly to the test,
And turned and were caught at the throat and chest.

They took the lunge as if their fire could grate
The awkward stone-boat forward like a feather,
Staggered under the impact of dead weight,
Like shackled furies almost knelt together,
Huge haunches quivering under the jolt—
And spent their lightning in a single bolt.

The small men who had cursed and lashed out—
Dwarfs bending gods to their little will—
Gentled them to a walk and led them out,
Set free again—but oh, they trembled still!—

While judges measured the courage of their bound
In hard-won inches on the battleground.

We watched this act repeated there for hours,
As some teams failed, and all grew more tense,
Stone piled on stone to strain utmost powers;
At last the weight was cruel and immense,
Our favorites winning to the last assay,
Cheered as they danced in, still relaxed and gay.

Win or lose now, we stood on our bench
To cheer this final test, as the brute force
Burst against dead weight in a violent wrench
Of nerve and muscle. The attack was fierce,
But spent too soon. They buckled to their knees,
And lost the day, heads bent upon the frieze.

The failure seemed some inward-fated doom:
How could they win, or we, who had given
Our hearts to horses all that afternoon?
We left, unnerved, and came shadowed home,
Thinking of all who strive and lose their grip,
And of wild hopes, and of the tragic slip.

May Sarton

The stall so tight he can't raise heels or knees
when the cowboy, coccyx to bareback, touches down

tender as a deerfly, forks him, gripping the rope-
handle over the withers, testing the cinch,

as if hired to lift a cumbersome piece of brown
luggage, while assistants perched on the rails arrange

the kicker, a foam-rubber band around the narrowest,
most ticklish part of the loins, leaning full weight

on neck and rump to keep him throttled, this horse,
"Firecracker," jacked out of the box through the sprung

gate, in the same second raked both sides of the belly
by ratchets on booted heels, bursts into five-way

motion: bucks, pitches, swivels, humps, and twists,
an all-over-body-sneeze that must repeat

until the flapping bony lump attached to his spine is gone.
A horn squawks. From the dust gets up a buster named Tucson.

May Swenson

Stewball was a good horse
He wore a high head
And the mane on his foretop
Was fine as silk thread

I rode him in England
I rode him in Spain
He never did lose, boys
He always did gain

So come all you gamblers
Wherever you are
And don't bet your money
On that little grey mare

Most likely she'll stumble
Most likely she'll fall
But you never will lose, boys
On my noble Stewball

As they were a-riding
'Bout halfway around
That grey mare she stumbled
And fell to the ground

And away out yonder
Ahead of them all
Came a prancin' and a dancin'
My noble Stewball

Irish Folk Song

For Maxine Kumin

He sees the light cart in the paddock,
isn't thinking of the time he spooked a month ago—
the cart half-hitched, the gate unlocked—
and you held on. Today, he's calm,

standing quietly as you thread the traces through the
footman's loop and ask him to back up. I stand
by his Arab head, masked in mosquito netting, and then
join you in the seat that substitutes, today, for his back.

Easy in your hands, he trots up the road, ears alert
to your voice, the encouraging praise, the clucks that urge him
past laziness when the hill steepens. Your hands know
the give and take of the canter, the sweet compromise

that adjudicates his power and your will. In our helmets,
under these summer trees, we are as safe as we will ever be.

Robin Becker

I want to say something
about Nance and Birdie,
two horses that I rode
bareback with my grand-
father's help when I
was a child growing up
in southern Indiana.
At sixty now I still feel
the slide of knobby spine,
short legs barely spread
over broad flanks as I
gripped two-fisted reins
of mane while my grand-
father walked alongside
talking strange syllables
he said was horse talk,
his spotted hands holding
the real reins, leather
stained dark with sweat.

(I don't remember which
was Birdie, which Nance,
no distinguishing marks.
Both were roan mares,
workhorses pulling a plow
that cut furrows for planting
corn and sorghum. Kept
in a tin-roofed barn that housed
a small silo, they stomped
and shivered in their stalls,
and what I remember
even more than their size
is the smell of leather mixed
with hay and the sharp air
of the chicken coop nearby.)

We always rode twice
around the pond, the muddy
edges moon-scaped
with crayfish holes,
then stopped for a drink
as I squeezed leg-tight
to keep from sliding down
that length of neck into water
yellow as horse teeth.
Back at the barn, I was
scooped to the ground, told
to walk up the path a bit
where hollyhocks towered
over the garden fence
while my grandfather led
Nance or Birdie to her stall,
dark though streaked with light
slicing weathered boards.
At the farmhouse there would
be questions, adults waiting
as I struggled, then as now,
for the grace of good words.

Roger Pfingston

V. MIRRORS

. . . ephemeral horses
sewn from dreamskin and old chants
—Edgar Silex, "Blue Cloud Rides Horses"

the sun over the horizon
a sweating yellow horse
our continuance
        the unaccountable distance
that sweeps through our hands
the first prayers
        in the morning
it is this that i believe in
the galloping sun
and my whole life
        a rider

        Joy Harjo

Perhaps the ankle of a horse is holy.

Crossing the Mississippi at dusk, Clemens thought
Of a sequel in which Huck Finn, in old age, became
A hermit, & insane. And never wrote it.

And perhaps all that he left out is holy.

The river, anyway, became a sacrament when
He spoke of it, even though
The last ten chapters were a failure he devised

To please America, & make his lady
Happy: to buy her silk, furs, & jewels with

Hues no one in Hannibal had ever seen.

There, above the river, if
The pattern of the stars is a blueprint for a heaven
Left unfinished,

I also believe the ankle of a horse,
In the seventh furlong, is as delicate as the fine lace
Of faith, & therefore holy.

I think it was only Twain's cynicism, the smell of a river
Lingering in his nostrils forever, that kept
His humor alive to the end.

I don't know how he managed it.

I used to make love to a woman, who,
When I left, would kiss the door she held open for me,
As if instead of me, as if she already missed me.
I would stand there in the cold air, breathing it,
Amused by her charm, which was, like the scent of a river,

Provocative, the dusk & first lights along the shore.
Should I say my soul went mad for a year, &
Could not sleep? To whom should I say so?

She was gentle, & intended no harm.

If the ankle of a horse is holy, & if it fails
In the stretch & the horse goes down, &
The jockey in the bright shout of his silks
Is pitched headlong onto
The track, & maimed, & if, later, the horse is
Destroyed, & all that is holy

Is also destroyed: hundreds of bones & muscles that
Tried their best to be pure flight, a lyric
Made flesh, then

I would like to go home, please.

Even though I betrayed it, & left, even though
I might be, at such a time as I am permitted
To go back to my wife, my son—no one, or

No more than a stone in a pasture full
Of stones, full of the indifferent grasses,

(& Huck Finn insane by then & living alone)

It will be, it might be still,
A place where what can only remain holy grazes, &
Where men might, also, approach with soft halters,
And, having no alternative, lead that fast world

Home—though it is only to the closed dark of stalls,
And though the men walk ahead of the horses slightly
Afraid, & at all times in awe of their
Quickness, & how they have nothing to lose, especially

Now, when the first stars appear slowly enough
To be counted, & the breath of horses makes white signatures

On the air: *Last Button, No Kidding, Brief Affair*—

And the air is colder.

                                              Larry Levis

Horses gallop over the vast plain.
Going where?
Going to look for the head of the Dauphin that is
    rolling down the stairs.
The spirited horses shake out their long blue manes.
One holds in his teeth the dead white actress he drew
    from the waters,
Others carry the wind's message to vanished explorers,
Others carry wheat to people abandoned by their leaders.
The lean blue horses whinny toward the airplane,
Pound the hard earth with their shining hooves.
They are the last of an old race, man's companion.
He will replace them with mechanical horses
And throw them off into the abyss of history.
The impatient blue horses have closed off the curve
    of the horizon,
Wakening trumpets in the dawn.

                                   Murilo Mendes
                          Translated by W. S. Merwin

She had some horses.

She had horses who were bodies of sand.
She had horses who were maps drawn of blood.
She had horses who were skins of ocean water.
She had horses who were the blue air of sky.
She had horses who were fur and teeth.
She had horses who were clay and would break.
She had horses who were splintered red cliff.

She had some horses.

She had horses with long, pointed breasts.
She had horses with full, brown thighs.
She had horses who laughed too much.
She had horses who threw rocks at glass houses.
She had horses who licked razor blades.

She had some horses.

She had horses who danced in their mother's arms.
She had horses who thought they were the sun and their
bodies shone and burned like stars.
She had horses who waltzed nightly on the moon.
She had horses who were much too shy, and kept quiet
in stalls of their own making.

She had some horses.

She had horses who liked Creek Stomp Dance songs.
She had horses who cried in their beer.
She had horses who spit at male queens who made
them afraid of themselves.
She had horses who said they weren't afraid.
She had horses who lied.
She had horses who told the truth, who were stripped
bare of their tongues.

She had some horses.

She had horses who called themselves, "horse."
She had horses who called themselves, "spirit," and kept
their voices secret and to themselves.
She had horses who had no names.
She had horses who had books of names.

She had some horses.

She had horses who whispered in the dark, who were afraid to speak.
She had horses who screamed out of fear of the silence, who
carried knives to protect themselves from ghosts.
She had horses who waited for destruction.
She had horses who waited for resurrection.

She had some horses.

She had horses who got down on their knees for any savior.
She had horses who thought their high price had saved them.
She had horses who tried to save her, who climbed in her
bed at night and prayed as they raped her.

She had some horses.

She had some horses she loved.
She had some horses she hated.

These were the same horses.

Joy Harjo

i once knew a man who had wild horses killed.
when he told about it
the words came galloping out of his mouth
and shook themselves and headed off in
every damn direction. his tongue
was wild and wide and spinning when he talked
and the people he looked at closed their eyes
and tore the skins off their backs as they walked away
and stopped eating meat.
there was no holding him once he got started;
he had had wild horses killed one time and
they rode him to his grave.

Lucille Clifton

I wake in New Hampshire.
The sun is still withheld.
For six days Amanda has stood
through drizzles and downpours.

This morning she steams.
Little pyramids of her droppings
surround her. Dead worms
shine in them like forgotten

spaghetti, proof she has eaten
the sugar-coated cure.
Four dozen ascarids, ten strongyles—
I count them to make sure.

And all the while in Washington
worms fall out of the government
pale as the parasites that drain
from the scoured gut of my mare.

They blink open on the television screen.
Night after night on the re-run
I count them to make sure.

                                        Maxine Kumin

Blue Cloud Rides Horses

For cousin-brother Mandis

blue cloud rides horses behind the wheel
of his chevy el camino with the hurst
four-on-the-floor

blue cloud rides psychedelic horses
and some made of remembered pain

blue cloud rides horses that leave hoof trails
up and down his atrophic veins

blue cloud rides cellblock horses
made of steel bars and thick walls
and when he gets out he rides horses again

blue cloud rides his baby's horse
and it makes him cry and it makes him cry
and it makes him want to forget
and makes him want and want and nearly die of want

blue cloud rides horses he thinks he hates
named officer   custer   john smith
de soto   jefferson   jackson   lincoln
columbus   cortez   and BIA

blue cloud rides horses he remembers he loved
named gin for the father he loved
named wild irish rose for the mother he loved

blue cloud rides ephemeral horses
sewn from dreamskin and old chants
named blue cloud and red cloud and white cloud
and grey clouds that rain faded dreams

blue cloud rides wind war-horses
on the ghost breezes
of the little big horn's plains
and he always wins   and he always wins

blue cloud rides horses that ride him
harder and faster to the vanishing haze

Edgar Silex

She is like a horse grazing
a hill pasture that someone makes
smaller by coming every night
to pull the fences in and in.

She has stopped running wide loops,
stopped even the tight circles.
She drops her head to feed; grass
is dust, and the creekbed's dry.

Master, come with your light
halter. Come and bring her in.

Jane Kenyon

Sometimes the
green pasture
of the mind
tilts abruptly.
The grazing horses
struggle crazily
for purchase
on the frictionless
nearly vertical
surface. Their
furniture-fine
legs buckle
on the incline,
unhorsed by slant
they weren't
designed to climb
and can't.

Kay Ryan

These are the ones who escape
after the last hurt is turned inward;
they are the most dangerous ones.
These are the hottest ones,
but so cold that your tongue sticks
to them and is torn apart because it is
frozen to the motion of hooves.
These are the ones who cut your thighs,
whose blood you must have seen on the gloves
of the doctor's rubber hands. They are
the horses who moaned like oceans, and
one of them a young woman screamed aloud;
she was the only one.
These are the ones who have found you.
These are the ones who pranced on your belly.
They chased deer out of your womb.
These are the ice horses, horses
who entered through your head,
and then your heart.
your beaten heart.

These are the ones who loved you.
They are the horses who have held you
so close that you have become
a part of them,
                        an ice horse
galloping into
                  the fire.

Joy Harjo

2

There is in every animal's eye a dim image and gleam of
humanity, a flash of strange light through which their life
looks out and up to our great mystery of command over
them.
—John Ruskin

She would not see them as subservient.
She painted the tarsal joint of the hind leg
for forty years, perfecting its voluted spring.
She knew the Arabian horse to be of porphyry, granite,
    and sandstone;
she knew the English stallion Hobgoblin, veined with seawater.
She knew anatomical science predicted movement;
thus, in trousers and boots, through the slaughterhouses and
    stockyards
and livestock markets, a small woman with cropped hair passed.
She knew the Belgian, her dense ossature, wattage of the livid eye,
oscillation of gait, the withheld stampede gathering
in the staunch shoulder for the haulage of artillery.
She would not picture subservience.

    [. . .]

8

Now I am turned 73 and have only one tooth left wherewith
to snarl at humanity.
—Rosa Bonheur

Nine horses running in a cadenced score,
their unshod hooves thresh the wheat and the thresher's whip
like a high note on the unfinished canvas.

An immense dream of balance, gallop, and pivot—
without bridle or harness—
the picture hung for thirty years in the atelier.

She wanted to show the fire that blows
from the horses' nostrils, and the driven herd mutinous, rising
and falling along the enclosure of the thresher's will

into the foundry of weight and motion
where metal melts and pours into horse.
Dangerous as fission the arson of their turning;

tails flare behind obdurate haunches, chests brace in disavowal.
She painted the intelligence of dished faces resisting—
her life's project their refusal.

                                                    Robin Becker

On Looking at Stubbs's "Anatomy of the Horse"

In Lincolnshire, a village full of tongues
Not tired by a year's wagging, and a man
Shut in a room where a wrecked carcass hangs,
His calm knife peeling putrid flesh from bone.
He whistles softly, as an ostler would;
The dead horse moves, as if it understood.

That night a yokel holds the taproom still
With tales new-hatched; he's peeped, and seen a mare
Stand there alive with naked rib and skull—
The creature neighed, and stamped upon the floor;
The warlock asked her questions, and she spoke;
He wrote her answers down in a huge book.

Two centuries gone, I have the folio here,
And turn the pages, find them pitiless.
These charts of sinew, vein and bone require
A glance more expert, more detached than this—
Fingering the margins, I think of the old
Sway-backed and broken nags the pictures killed.

Yet, standing in that room, I watch the knife;
Light dances on it as it maps a joint
Or scribes a muscle; I am blank and stiff
The blade cuts so directly to my want;
I gape for anecdote, absurd detail,
Like any yokel with his pint of ale.

Edward Lucie-Smith

*(Artist Martin Anderson built a series of neon horses which appeared
in fields along the I-5 throughout Oregon.)*

To come upon one, driving toward your lover
in the dark, the highway steaming
under four grooved wheels, the dry hum
of roadside weeds, cigarette smoke's
ribbon wisped out the open wind wing,
radio low, shadow of some small creature
careening alongside the interstate.

To look up and see one grazing in a field,
serene, calm as the moon in the severed dark,
bright hooves sunk in black nightgrass,
head dipped like a spoon to a pool of earth,
delicate spine glowing, blue bridge
arched to the stars, tail stroke throwing off
ghost light, empty haunch through which
the sagebrush, windswept, sways.

To see, for miles, its burning shape,
barest outline of throat, foreleg, the imagined
fetlock brushed in. The surprise of horse
held like breath, horse and what horse means
gleaming like a constellation, lineaments
of the true world: cowbird and sugar cube,
fallen apple, tractor wheel, torn wheat
in its worn treads, silo, hay, the baled sky, ruffled pond
from which geese, squalling, lift.

The after smell of horse, rising, feral,
floating above the sorrel. The way night
knows itself with roses and thorns, buried edges,
knowing his arms are down there, electric, spread,
his jaw lifted to the kiss on its way, depth
to be met and entered, full on his lips, moving toward it,

a still joy hovering behind the eyes:
as when the living horse is seen,
incomparable, massive, universe
of horse, too much for the mind,
only the heart's dark world can hold it,
crucible moment, muscle greeting muscle,
grass, gallop, crushed blossom, intake
of voltage, blue horse of the valley, horse
of dream, lit chimera distilled from liquid air.

Dorianne Laux

Horse in Amsterdam, after Rembrandt

If I could read the blazed face
of this huge horse at night
with its hair like black flame
and its eyes charred chestnuts
I would want for words to tell
of the deeps drowned there
and the dumb world muted there
where the souls of dark trees
raise their raving arms
And nothing stops the stoned night
in the wilderness of its eyes

Lawrence Ferlinghetti

Penciled creases, fine runnels
as the neck swings, head arcs . . .

Palm muscle's curve, power:
outlines of thrust, veering and return,
speed's contours defining the vein-
patterned pelt.

Shape and space between sounds: bridle
rattle, turf-crop and slow munch,
the percussive canter, leap's
sudden silence.

A creased bougainvillea calyx,
crisp coral tinge, contrasts

thud's umber resonance
in dark and hay-strewn stable,
a whinny's descending spiral,
iron's looped density: horseshoes
along splintering beam.

Trace mane's texture
and high tail's sweep, nostril-soft
flare, the sloping limber
hush of shoulder, flank; a swift
drop to fetlock, the done of hoof.

Jenny Kander

The painted caballos of the carnival
have been covered for the night. Under
that black cloth they gallop still,
hard around the mirrored dark, circling
the small gold lights to the organ's
wheezy tune, and always on their backs
the warm hands of niños, their chubby legs
gripping as though the caballos were going
somewhere wild, beyond the earshot
of criadas, gossiping in the back patio,
to places their parents can never know
who think the children safe in bed
when they've kissed their drowsy
cheeks goodnight, and shut the door.

Lola Haskins

The Horse in the Drugstore

wants to be admired.
He no longer thinks of what he has given up
to stand here, the milk-white reason
of chickens over his head in the night, the grass
spilling on through the day. No, it is enough
to stand so with his polished chest among the nipples
and bibs, the cotton, and multiple sprays, with his black lips
parted just slightly and the forehooves doubled back
in the lavender air. He has learned when maligned to snort
dimes and to carry the inscrutable bruise like a bride.

Tess Gallagher

Don't let that horse
                          eat that violin

    cried Chagall's mother

                            But he
            kept right on
                            painting

And became famous

And kept on painting
                        The Horse With Violin In Mouth
And when he finally finished it
he jumped up upon the horse
                            and rode away
            waving the violin

And then with a low bow gave it
to the first naked nude he ran across

And there were no strings
                        attached

                        Lawrence Ferlinghetti

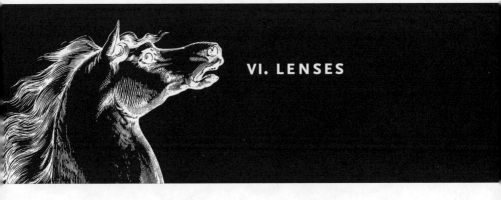

And the soaring of the prairies depends absolutely

On the wings of the ponies . . .

—Pattiann Rogers, "Naked Boys on Naked Ponies"

When I was thirteen I found two horses.
The shining one calls itself, *Keeper of Lights*.
The wild one calls itself, *Never Tame Me*.

Keeper of Lights comes when I call her
from the stable at the end of the world
hung with bridles and bits so soft
a rose might wear them and love the journey.

Never Tame Me shies at the sight of a saddle,
bare as a wave with her rocking gait
when we gallop on the dark meadows.
The rim of the sea is her fence.

One carries me home, the other shadows her
on the slippery trail shifting and shaking
where even a river could lose its way

between sleeping and waking.

                                        Nancy Willard

Two southern horses dreamed
of a snowstorm shutting the door

Their master slept
like a bear in winter

In the evening the mare
gave birth to a black pony

but the master didn't come
swinging a lantern in his hand

and the three horses
flew across the snow plains

three stars shining
distant

By morning the marks
of their hooves were effaced

Xi Chuan
Translated by Tony Barnstone and the poet

We are riding.
The wheels of the wagon
run around the moon.
The footprints of the horse
measure out dreams,
dreams
of the frightened birch trees
that fled from warm homes
to lonely roads.

Quiet.
Sleeping dogs.
From empty pails
silence drips down
into deep wells.
We are riding.
On a doorstep of a dark cottage
stands a woman—
motionless,
in a white shirt.

                    (Gombin, 1933)

            Rajzel Zychlinsky
        Translated by Barnett Zumoff

Its face, as long as an arm, looks down & down.
Then the iron gate sound of the cage swings shut
above the bed, a bell as big as the room: quarter-
moon of the head, its nose, its whole lean body
pressed against its cell . . .
I watched my father hit a horse in the face once.
It had come down to feed across the fence.
My father, this stranger, wanted to ride.
Perhaps he only wanted to talk. Anyway,
he hit the ground and something broke.
As a child I never understood how an animal
could sleep standing. In my dream the horse
rocks in a cage too small, so the cage swings.
I still wake up dreaming, in front of a long face.
That day I hugged the ground hard.
Who knows if my heartbroken father was meant
to last longer than his last good drunk.
They say it's like being kicked by a horse.
You go down, your knees hug up.
You go suddenly wide awake, and the gate shuts.

Stanley Plumly

White Horse of the Father, White Horse of the Son

For Michael Perry

Not the delicate mare who came nosing.
Not the dustdim ironeyed gelding.
This was the one. The bright dancer
who would not approach the fence.

Set in this side of his snowbright face
was the blank blue stare of the sky.
And there in the other, a hazel tunnel.
A swirling of greens and browns that could see.

The hooves were pink as tea-roses,
streaked with the pale of oystershell.
This was the great horse I wanted.
And this was the one for sale!

I wanted to try him alone.
How many moons has the sky?
You insisted my friend ride him too.
And he didn't know how. Didn't know.

My hands crossed the brilliant silk
of his neck as the lips of a prince cross
the princess. Who sleeps in forever.
Who wakes in the world. He woke

to my touch and we raced the proud wind
over grass. Over bushes and ditches.
This was the one, the one my dreams
woke to. Wide-eyed. But my friend,

I could feel him slipping.
Feel him falling back into the grass
as I reached, too late, for his hand.
As my hand reached backward into the blur

of his wide white face and the grass.
He was gone. By the time I could turn
I had heard your voice in my heart.
No Sir. Not this one. No sale.

Father once a son, son become a father,
you riding now the white stallion of your bones!
It is true that I fell from the horse as your son.
That I rode on. Am still riding.

William Pitt Root

They ride through invisible hollows
And along the indefinite edges of marshy streams,
Fog swirling up to their ears
Over beds of sida and flowering spurge.
The ponies' withers become ivory with pollen
From the blossoming quince, and the bare
Legs of the boys are marked by flickertail
Barley and wild mint. Moisture
On the corn cockle along the ridges
Makes constant suns in their eyes.

Galloping through forests and across fields
Of drying grasses, this is what they create
By themselves—spilled ginseng and screeching
Pitpits, dusts rising from the withered
And the wild raisin, an effusion of broken
Beargrass somersaulting skyward
And mouse-ear chickweed kicked high.

And beside the river they see themselves
On the opposite bank following themselves
Through water chestnuts and willow oak, and they see
Themselves threading among the stand of hornbeam
In the forest ahead. Watching from the precipice
Above the canyon at evening, they know the bronze
Ponies and their riders curving in a line
Along the ledges below.

And at night they see themselves riding upside down
Across the sky, hair and tails and manes
Dragging in the grasses among the long horn beetles
And burrowing owls. And they see themselves galloping
Across the prairie turned upside down, hair
And tails and manes dragging in the dusty glow
Of the starry nebulae. They know they are the definite
Wish of all unexplored spaces to be ponies and boys.

I tell you the speed of the ponies depends absolutely
On the soaring of the rider squeezing tightly

Inside each of their skulls. And the wings of the boys
Depend absolutely on the flight of the ponies
Galloping across the prairies contained in their bones.
And the soaring of the prairies depends absolutely
On the wings of the ponies squeezing tightly
Inside every grass and bone found in the flight of the boys.

And who cares where they are going,
And who cares if they are real or not,
When their ride by itself is that glorious?

Pattiann Rogers

In bright morning sunlight, the horse appears pink,
and the man is so pleased to see it that he waves
as he walks toward it across the triangular field.
The horse glances up from between two apple trees
and waits. The man was awakened early by dreams of
winter and self-doubt, dreams of no money in the bank;
and now he wants to clear his head by galloping bareback
through summer lanes with dust billowing around him,
light flickering around him in a hundred shades of green.
And he decides to gallop so fast that all the impediments
and small debts of his life will be lost in a swirl
of debris, that even his own death which he thinks
must be as gnarled as the trunks of surrounding trees
will be left deserted and despairing in the middle
of some sun-choked lane.   As he walks toward the horse,
he anticipates the swell of its body beneath him,
pushing out his thighs as he lies with heels pressed
against its belly, urging it to gallop even faster.
And he's sorry he can't take this back to the city:
simply, the flickering light and smell of summer grasses.
Then, in winter, when he and the world fought one another
and he gnawed at himself, was cruel to people around him,
he would think of the morning he galloped the pink horse
between apple trees, and the world fitted together
without angry words and extra pieces, and across
the lurching sky he saw his own name hastily scrawled
as if on an IOU from somebody notoriously disreputable,
someone who has never been known to tell the truth,
but who for the brief moment he has chosen to believe.

Stephen Dobyns

Right under their noses, the green
Of the field is paling away
Because of something fallen from the sky.

They see this, and put down
Their long heads deeper in grass
That only just escapes reflecting them

As the dream of a millpond would.
The color green flees over the grass
Like an insect, following the red sun over

The next hill. The grass is white.
There is no cloud so dark and white at once;
There is no pool at dawn that deepens

Their faces and thirsts as this does.
Now they are feeding on solid
Cloud, and, one by one,

With nails as silent as stars among the wood
Hewed down years ago and now rotten,
The stalls are put up around them.

Now if they lean, they come
On wood on any side. Not touching it, they sleep.
No beast ever lived who understood

What happened among the sun's fields,
Or cared why the color of grass
Fled over the hill while he stumbled,

Led by the halter to sleep
On his four taxed, worthy legs.
Each thinks he awakens where

The sun is black on the rooftop,
That the green is dancing in the next pasture,
And that the way to sleep

In a cloud, or in a risen lake,
Is to walk as though he were still
In the drained field standing, head down,

136

To pretend to sleep when led,
And thus to go under the ancient white
Of the meadow, as green goes

And whiteness comes up through his face
Holding stars and rotten rafters,
Quiet, fragrant, and relieved.

James Dickey

There are hundreds of ways to keep warm.

Think igloos: all that hot ice.
Think fur, fat, fire,
straw in the barn, down on the swan.

Think the chimney poking upward
through this 1890 house,
which was, they say, a leather factory
once, with small rooms and linoleum
floors and horsehair insulation in the walls.

I know it's still there, even before
the painter tears down
three layers of wallpaper
and a big plaster crumble exposes
a round inch of red tail.

I touch the hair, soothe
the fretful racer who broke
her leg, the stubborn draft horse
seventeen hands high who dragged
blocks of stone wherever he was told.
I knock and a nicker goes up, soft and ancient.
A palm rubbed flat against the wall
gets a rough lick.

Nothing is truly lifeless.
Wood and stone buzz with atoms
of remembered form: star or tree.
A stalk of flax shivers in a linen shirt.
So, too, this Temple and Dungeon of Horse,
this factory-house where a horse could be reborn
into leather, glue and warmth.

Two months here, I have adopted
the house's heart, its gait.
I listen for the clang of a bell
to tell me when the long trough
will be filled, so I might lift
my long and gleaming head,
so I might quiver standing still.

Jean Monahan

from "Sitting in a Small Screenhouse on a Summer Morning"

Ten more miles, it is South Dakota.
Somehow, the roads there turn blue,
When no one walks down them.
One more night of walking, and I could have become
A horse, a blue horse, dancing
Down a road, alone.
[. . .]
It is so still now, I hear the horse
Clear his nostrils.
He has crept out of the green places behind me.
Patient and affectionate, he reads over my shoulder
These words I have written.
He has lived a long time, and he loves to pretend
No one can see him.
Last night I paused at the edge of darkness,
And slept with green dew, alone.
I have come a long way, to surrender my shadow
To the shadow of a horse.

James Wright

This morning, out early, I was confronted
by horses—two, then four—
coming from nowhere, head-high
along the street, their rhythmic pacing
and muscled sheen of hips and hocks
making patterns—dance drama
with sunlight—shrinking houses and hedges
till the whole block burgeoned out
into foothills, ranges and tussocky plains.

Behind them came the shadows
of little long-ago ponies,
noses into the wind, rough-coated
brumbies wearing their last freedom
galloping down ridges and away
over the wind-whistling plateau
of Tauranga-Taupo, more than
half a hundred years ago.

Lauris Edmond

In a dead tree
there is the ghost of a horse
no horse
was ever seen near the tree
but the tree was born
of a mare
it rolled with long legs
in rustling meadows
it pricked its ears
it reared and tossed its head
and suddenly stood still
beginning to remember
as its leaves fell

W. S. Merwin

The mounted horse will stop.
The decrepit porch will flinch.
The balcony's glass pane
will deform the face of the guard.

And the rider will hold his hand out
straight toward the rusty lock.
The horse in terror will draw away,
forsaken reins across its back.

He will gallop ever onward
on the trail of the unset sun.
Over makeshift pontoon bridges
he will cross the whirlpool.

For life's sake, for a word's sake,
for the sake of fish, of beasts, of men,
for the sake of a bloodshot eye—
the eye of his own horse.

Varlam Shalamov
Translated by Bradley Jordan

The silence of a place where there were once horses
is a mountain

and I have seen by lightning that every mountain
once fell from the air
ringing
like the chime of an iron shoe

high on the cloudy slope
riders who long ago abandoned sadness
leaving its rotting fences and its grapes to fall
have entered the pass
and are gazing into the next valley

I do not see them cross over

I see that I will be lying
in the lightning on an alp of death
and out of my eyes horsemen will be riding

W. S. Merwin

In the middle of the thunder of the abyss,
the dense kernel of silence. Silence more vast
than the forests of death:
Silence Itself.
And if you listen to this stillness, you will know
that in its core a pounding can be heard, like the rhythm
of a poem never uttered by anyone.

It is the hoofbeat of the white horse
bringing you the news for which you've waited so very long.

But if you remain completely deaf so as to listen to
the rhythmic clip-clop like your heart,
you will hear the Thunder, the explosion of worlds,
the roaring laughter of the great Logos in space . . .
Of which the dense kernel is silence.

Oh, it is the hoofbeat of the white horse
bringing you the news for which you've waited so very long.

Mihai Ursachi
Translated by Adam J. Sorkin

Guillaume Apollinaire, born in Italy in 1880, coined the term *surrealism* and wrote
prose fiction, drama, and librettos, but he is said to have published only two
significant works during his lifetime: *Alcools: Poèmes 1898–1913* and *Calligrammes:
Poèmes de la paix et de la guerre 1913–1916*. He died in 1918.

David Baker teaches at Denison University and is poetry editor of the *Kenyon Review*.
His most recent book is *Midwest Eclogue*.

Tony Barnstone is Faculty Master and associate professor of English at Whittier
College. He is the author of a book of poetry, *Impure*, a chapbook of poems, *Naked
Magic*, and has edited and/or translated several books of Chinese poetry and prose.
He has won an Artists Fellowship from the California Arts Council, as well as
many national poetry awards.

Willis Barnstone is a Guggenheim fellow, a Pulitzer Prize finalist in poetry, and
distinguished professor at Indiana University. His publications include *Modern
European Poetry*, *The Other Bible*, *The Secret Reader: 501 Sonnets*, *To Touch the Sky*,
and a literary translation of the New Testament. Barnstone has translated
numerous works of Rainer Maria Rilke.

Robin Becker, professor of English and women's studies at Pennsylvania State
University, has published five collections of poems. She has received individual
fellowships from the Bunting Institute, the Massachusetts Cultural Council, and
the NEA. Active as a book reviewer and judge for national poetry awards, Becker
serves as poetry editor for the *Women's Review of Books*.

Ben Belitt, author of *This Scribe My Hand, The Complete Poems of Ben Belitt*, translated
all of Pablo Neruda's major works.

Vizma Belševica, 1931–2005, Latvian poet, fiction writer, and translator, was the first
recipient of the Tomas Transtromer Prize for poetry (Sweden) in 1998 and a
longstanding nominee for the Nobel Prize in Literature.

Ernest Bernhardt-Kabisch is professor emeritus of English and comparative literature
at Indiana University, Bloomington. He has publications on English and European
romanticism and is a translator (from German) of numerous radio plays, essays,
and TV documentaries and articles for *Der Spiegel* magazine.

Linda Bierds received the PEN/West Poetry Prize and the Washington State
Governor's Writers Award for *The Profile Makers*, her fifth book of poetry.
Numerous other prizes include two grants from the NEA, three Pushcart Prizes,
and a number of fellowships. Her poems have appeared in numerous publications,
and she currently directs the creative writing program at the University of
Washington.

Paul Boldt, 1885–1921, studied German, art history, and later, medicine. He published numerous expressionistic and often erotic poems in the expressionist magazine *Die Aktion* and in his volume *Junge Pferde! Junge Pferde!*

Alison Brackenbury, English poet and librarian, has published five books of poetry as well as poems in a number of anthologies. She has had her work read on BBC Radio channels 3 and 4. She has won the Eric Gregory Award and the Cholmondely Award.

Gwendolyn Brooks, 1917–2000, is the author of more than twenty books of poetry, including *Annie Allen*, for which she received the Pulitzer Prize in 1949. She also wrote many other books, including a novel and an autobiography, and edited *Jump Bad: A New Chicago Anthology*. In 1968 she was named poet laureate for the State of Illinois, and from 1985 to 1986 she was consultant in poetry to the Library of Congress. Brooks was the recipient of numerous awards, including an NEA award and fellowships from the Academy of American Poets and the Guggenheim Foundation.

Lucille Clifton has authored a memoir, more than sixteen books for children, and more than nine books of poetry, a number of which were nominated for or won prizes. Further honors include two fellowships from the NEA and an Emmy Award from the American Academy of Television Arts and Sciences. In 1999 she was elected a chancellor of the Academy of American Poets, and she has served as poet laureate for the State of Maryland. She is distinguished professor of humanities at St. Mary's College of Maryland.

Pablo Antonio Cuadra, 1912–2002, Nicaraguan poet, essayist, critic, playwright, and graphic artist, often wrote about the identity of the Nicaraguans and of Latin America and was a vocal supporter of the poor and oppressed. He was codirector of the newspaper *La Prensa* and edited the influential journal *El Pez y La Serpiente*. Little of his poetry is available in English translation, the exception being *The Birth of the Sun: Selected Poems, 1935–1985.*

Babette Deutsch, 1895–1982, an American poet whose best-known collections include *Animal, Vegetable, Mineral, Coming of Age*, and *Collected Poems*, also wrote novels and numerous critical works, such as *Poetry in Our Time*.

James Dickey, 1923–1997, authored thirty books of poetry, several collections of essays, and three novels, the best known being *Deliverance*. From 1966 to 1968 Dickey served as poetry consultant to the Library of Congress. Among his several awards were a Guggenheim fellowship, a National Book Award, and the Medicis Prize. Honorary degrees were conferred upon him by thirteen American universities.

Stephen Dobyns has published ten books of poems, most recently *Pallbearers Envying the One Who Rides*, twenty-one works of fiction, and a book of essays on poetry, *Best*

Words, Best Order. His poems have won numerous awards and prizes; his novels have been translated into some fifteen languages, and two have been made into films. Dobyns has taught at many colleges and universities and is currently a contributing writer for the *San Diego Reader*.

Lauris Edmond, 1924–2000, a New Zealander, published twelve collections of poetry, an autobiography in three volumes, a novel, and a radio and stage drama. She received an OBE for services to poetry and literature, and Massey University awarded her an honorary doctorate of literature. Edmond won many honors, including a lifetime achievement award at the Montana New Zealand book awards in 1999.

Theodore Enslin is the author of nine poetry publications, two plays, and an extended essay on Gustav Mahler. His awards include the Niemann Award in 1955 for his weekly newspaper column and the Hart Crane Award for *To Come, to Have Become*.

Francis Fawkes, 1720–1777, English poet and translator, was educated at Cambridge and then took orders. He translated Sappho, among other classics, modernized poems, and in addition to the elegy on Dobbin, was the author of two other poems, "Bramham Park" and "Partridge Shooting."

Lawrence Ferlinghetti, painter, poet, translator, and author of plays, fiction, art criticism, and essays, cofounded City Lights Bookstore in 1953 and, two years later, City Lights Publishing House. Author of numerous books of poetry and the recipient of a number of prestigious awards, Ferlinghetti was named San Francisco's poet laureate in 1998 and was elected to the American Academy of Arts and Letters in 2003.

Cola Franzen is translator of the poetry collection *Background Noise* and the prose collection *In the Image and Likeness*, both by Saúl Yurkievich. She was awarded the Harold Morton Landon Translation Award by the Academy of American Poets in 2000 for *Horses in the Air and Other Poems* by Jorge Guillén. In 2004 she received the Gregory Kolovakis Award from PEN American Center.

Tess Gallagher has published various essays, collections of short fiction, and seven books of poems. She collaborated with her husband, Raymond Carver, on a screenplay about Fyodor Dostoyevsky. She has won many awards, including a fellowship from the Guggenheim Foundation, and holds an honorary doctorate in humane letters from Whitman College. Gallagher has taught at numerous universities.

Jason S. Greer, 1969–1999, won the Sidney Cox Award for creative writing at Dartmouth and was finishing a novel at the time of his accidental death. His work included composition and translation of poems and stories in both Korean and English.

Donald Hall has published fifteen books of poetry, a number of them award winners, including *The One Day*, which received a Pulitzer Prize nomination. In addition to poetry, Hall has written nonfiction, children's books, plays, and several autobiographical works. He has edited more than two dozen textbooks and anthologies. Hall's many honors include two Guggenheim fellowships and the Ruth Lilly Poetry Prize. He served as poet laureate of New Hampshire from 1984 to 1989.

Joy Harjo, poet, performer, writer, and musician, has written seven books of poetry, her most recent being *How We Became Human, New and Selected Poems*. She coedited the anthology *Reinventing the Enemy's Language, Native Women's Writing of North America*. Her numerous poetry awards include the Lifetime Achievement Award from the Native Writers Circle of the Americas and the William Carlos Williams Award from the Poetry Society of America.

Jana Harris is an award-winning poet, novelist, short story writer, and essayist. Her poetry books include *The Dust of Everyday Life*, an epic poem of the Pacific Northwest, and *We Never Speak of It: Idaho-Wyoming Poems, 1889–90*. She teaches poetry writing on-line at the University of Washington and is founder and editor of *Switched-on Gutenberg*, one of the first on-line poetry journals of the English-speaking world.

Lola Haskins is on the faculty of Pacific Lutheran University's MFA program. Her most recent collections are *Desire Lines, New and Selected Poems, The Rim Benders*, and *Extranjera*. Among this poet's awards are the Iowa Poetry Prize, two NEA fellowships, four Florida State arts fellowships, and narrative poetry prizes from the *New England Review* and the *Southern Poetry Review*.

William Hathaway has authored more than seven books of poems, among them *Gymnast of Inertia* and *Sightseer*. He has taught for several years at Louisiana State University.

Imru' al-Qays, who died before 550, is the most celebrated of the pre-Islamic Arabic poets and author of the most famous of the seven Golden Odes, which according to tradition were suspended from the Ka`bah in Mecca. The life of Imru' al-Qays is shrouded in legend, but he is considered the inventor of the classical ode.

Bradley Jordan has translated numerous Russian poets and has taught at Union College in Schenectady, New York.

Jane Kenyon, 1947–1995, published four volumes of poetry and translated *Twenty Poems of Anna Akhmatova*. *A Hundred White Daffodils* contains her essays, interviews, newspaper columns, and other work. Her poems appeared in many magazines. In 1995 Kenyon became poet laureate of New Hampshire. Three books of her poetry were published after her death.

Yusef Komunyakaa has authored eleven volumes of poetry, including the Pulitzer
Prize–winning *Neon Vernacular*. He has won numerous other awards and prizes.
He taught first at the University of New Orleans, was a professor at Indiana
University for more than ten years, and in 1997 became a professor in the Council
of Humanities and Creative Writing at Princeton University. He was elected a
chancellor of the Academy of American Poets in 1999.

Ted Kooser, poet laureate of the United States from 2004 to 2006, is the author of ten
collections of poetry, including *Winter Morning Walks: One Hundred Postcards to
Jim Harrison*, winner of the 2001 Nebraska Book Award for poetry. His work has
appeared in a variety of magazines, textbooks, and anthologies. Among other
awards and distinctions, he has received two NEA fellowships in poetry, the
Pushcart Prize, the Stanley Kunitz Prize, the Society of Midland Authors Prize, and
a Merit Award from the Nebraska Arts Council. A book of prose, *Local Wonders:
Seasons in the Bohemian Alps*, has won numerous awards. His most recent book,
Delights and Shadows, is winner of the 2005 Pulitzer Prize for poetry. Kooser is a
visiting professor at the University of Nebraska, Lincoln.

Maxine Kumin is the author of more than thirteen books of poems, five novels, a
collection of short stories, four essay collections, and more than twenty children's
books. She has received numerous prizes, among them a Pulitzer Prize in poetry
and the Ruth Lilly Poetry Prize. She served as consultant in poetry to the Library
of Congress before the post was renamed poet laureate of the United States.
Kumin has taught at Princeton, Columbia, Brandeis, and Washington universities
and has given widespread readings and writers' workshops.

Labid ibn Rabi`ah, 560–660, is one of the poets of the Golden Odes of pre-Islamic
Arabic poetry, that is, the seven master poems that, according to tradition, were
suspended from the Ka`bah in Mecca. Born before the coming of Islam, Labîd
lived to see the Prophet Muhammad and convert. According to literary lore
he gave up composing poetry when he adopted Islam and therefore his Golden
Ode is considered a pre-Islamic work.

Philip Larkin, 1922–1985, English poet, novelist, critic, and librarian, is best known for
the books of poetry *The Less Deceived*, *The Whitsun Weddings*, and *High Windows*.
He also wrote jazz reviews for the *Daily Telegraph* and published one book of
essays.

Dorianne Laux is the author of *What We Carry*, a finalist for the National Book Critics
Circle Award, and three other volumes of poetry. She is coauthor, with Kim
Addonizio, of *The Poet's Companion: A Guide to the Pleasures of Writing Poetry*.
Her work has been published in a wide variety of magazines and in *The Norton
Anthology of Contemporary Poetry* and has been translated into French, Italian,

Korean, Romanian, and Portuguese. Among her awards are a Pushcart Prize for poetry, two NEA fellowships, and a Guggenheim fellowship. Laux is associate professor in the University of Oregon's Creative Writing Program.

Larry Levis, 1946–1996, wrote five volumes of poems, a book of short stories, and the collection *Elegy*, which was published posthumously. He taught at a number of universities and at the time of his death was professor of English at Virginia Commonwealth University. He received fellowships from the NEA and the Guggenheim Memorial Foundation and was selected for the National Poetry Series. In 1989 he was a senior Fulbright fellow in Yugoslavia.

Vachel Lindsay, 1879–1931, was a painter, poet, and balladeer who published six books of poetry. With Langston Hughes, he helped define the shape of jazz poetry in the early twentieth century. His style of poetry performance culminated in the recordings of the Beat generation.

Michael List, 1948–2005, founded Blue Sky Veterinary Clinic, at which he practiced equine and small-animal medicine for twenty-seven years. His poems appeared in regional publications around southern Indiana.

Henry Wadsworth Longfellow, 1807–1882, poet, storyteller, and translator, traveled widely and wrote narratives, epics, novels, a drama, and several poems on slavery. He taught at Harvard and was the most popular American poet of the nineteenth century. His best-known narrative poem is "The Song of Hiawatha."

Edward Lucie-Smith, born in Jamaica, is an internationally known English art critic and prolific historian. He is also a published poet, a member of the Académie Européenne de Poésie, a winner of the John Llewellyn Rhys Memorial Prize, an anthologist, and a practicing photographer.

Thomas Babington Macaulay, 1800–1859, English historian, author, and lawyer, was elected to Parliament in 1830. He wrote short biographical essays and the highly acclaimed five-volume *History of England from the Accession of James the Second*. "The Battle of Lake Regillus" is taken from his poetical work, *Lays of Ancient Rome*, which celebrates the great events of Roman history.

Linda McCarriston holds dual Irish and U.S.A. citizenship. She is the author of three highly acclaimed poetry collections, *Talking Soft Dutch*, an AWP Award Series Selection; *Eva-Mary*, winner of the 1991 Terrence Des Pres Prize; and the 1991 National Book Award finalist *Little River*. Her poems have appeared in a variety of anthologies. McCarriston has taught at the University of Alaska, Anchorage, since 1994.

Ann McCarthy de Zavala has a BA in Spanish literature from Smith College and an MA in Latin American studies from Georgetown University. While living in Nicaragua between 1971 and 1984, she was a close friend of Pablo Antonio Cuadra, who often clarified the meaning of his poems and helped with the translations. McCarthy de Zavala is currently vice president of Asociación Libro Libre, Escazu, Costa Rica.

Murilo Mendes, 1901–1975, poet, diplomat, and author of prose works and memoirs, played an important role in Brazilian modernism after 1930. He published twelve volumes of poems and in 1972 was the first Brazilian poet to win the Etna-Taormina International Poetry Prize. Much of his life was spent as cultural attaché in the Brazilian embassy in Italy and as professor of Brazilian literature at the University of Rome.

W. S. Merwin, with four books of prose, numerous plays, and more than fifteen volumes of poetry to his name, is also an essayist and translator of Latin, French, Spanish, and Japanese poetry, with nearly twenty books of translation. He has won the Yale Series of Younger Poets Award for 1952, a Pulitzer Prize, and the Lenore Marshall Poetry Prize. In 1999, his *The River Sound* was named a *New York Times* Notable Book of the Year.

Jean Monahan is the author of three books of poetry, one of which, *Hands*, was a winner of the 1991 Anhinga Prize. She is a recipient of several other awards, and her work has appeared in numerous journals and anthologies. She is a copywriter and Web producer.

Minnie Hite Moody, 1900–1993, novelist, poet, and journalist, wrote five novels, various short stories, and columns for the *Atlanta Journal*. Among other publications, her poems were published in the *Georgia Review* and the *Saturday Evening Post*. She received the Ohioana Library Career Medal—the highest honor of the Ohioana Library Association—in 1976.

Ilze Klavina Mueller, a former teacher and academic, has a PhD in German language and literature and has been translating from German and Latvian for many years. Her published translations include the poetry of Vizma Belševica, Latvian fiction, and five books on twentieth-century German film and modern architecture. She is a former recipient of a Jauna Gaita (Canada) translation award. Mueller's recent poetry has been collected in *Gate*.

Pablo Neruda, 1904–1973, born in Chile, is one of the greatest Spanish-language poets of the twentieth century. He wrote erotically charged love poems, poems on nature, surrealist poems, historical epics, and overtly political poems. In 1971 Neruda was awarded the Nobel Prize for literature.

Edward Parone, theatre and television director, was a book review editor at a publishing house in New York. He was also Edward Albee's play agent and a director both off Broadway and in Los Angeles at the Mark Taper Forum. Written during the fifties, many of his poems appeared in the *New Yorker*.

Roger Pfingston is a retired teacher of English and photography. His first collection of poems was *Something Iridescent*, and his most recent chapbooks are *Singing to the Garden* and *Earthbound*.

Stanley Plumly is distinguished university professor at the University of Maryland. His last two books are *Now That My Father Lies Down Beside Me: New and Selected Poems, 1970–2000* and *Argument and Song: Sources and Silences in Poetry*.

Rainer Maria Rilke, 1875–1926, is an Austrian poet whose most famous poems are *Duino Elegies* and *Sonnets to Orpheus*. Prior to these he published five volumes of poetry and, thereafter, another three collections.

Pattiann Rogers has published eleven books of poetry and several chapbooks. She has received two NEA awards, a Guggenheim fellowship, a Lannan Poetry fellowship, and four Pushcart Prizes. She has been a visiting writer at the universities of Texas, Montana, and Arkansas and a faculty member at Vermont College.

William Pitt Root has an eighth collection, *White Boots: New and Selected Poems of the American West*, which will appear in 2006. *The Storm and Other Poems* was released in Carnegie Mellon's Contemporary Classics series in 2005. *Trace Elements from a Recurring Kingdom* was a Nation Notable Book for 1994. Recent work appears in various magazines and in anthologies. Root has been a U.S./U.K. Exchange Artist as well as a fellow of the Rockefeller Foundation, the Guggenheim Foundation, Stanford University, and the NEA. He has taught at a number of colleges.

Kay Ryan has six books of poems, the last titled *The Niagara River*. She has been awarded fellowships from the Guggenheim Foundation, the NEA, and the Ingram-Merrill Foundation, and in 2004 she received the Ruth Lilly Poetry Prize.

Carl Sandburg, 1878–1967, a prolific poet who gained international acclaim, wrote poetry, nonfiction, children's stories, a novel, two volumes of folk songs, and an autobiography. He won two Pulitzer Prizes, the first in 1940 for *Abraham Lincoln: The War Years* (in four volumes) and the second in 1951 for his *Complete Poems*.

May Sarton, 1912–1995, naturalized American poet, was born in Belgium. She wrote novels, journals, poetry, essays on the art and craft of writing, and children's books—fifty-four volumes in all. Her collection of poetry *The Land of Silence* won the Reynolds Lyric Award, and her novel *Faithful Are the Wounds* and poetry book *In Time Like Air* had dual nominations in 1958 for the National Book Award. *Poetry Magazine* awarded Sarton the Levinson Prize for poetry in 1993, her eighty-first year.

Grace Schulman's latest books of poems are *Days of Wonder: New and Selected Poems* and *The Paintings of Our Lives*. She is the recipient of major awards, including a Guggenheim fellowship and the Aiken-Taylor Award for poetry. Schulman is distinguished professor at Baruch College, City University of New York.

Anne Sexton, 1928–1974, experienced quick success with her poetry after her first workshop, with poems accepted by the *New Yorker, Harper's Magazine,* and the *Saturday Review.* She taught workshops at Boston College, Oberlin College, and Colgate University. The modern model of the confessional poet, Sexton helped open the door for female poets and female issues, redefining the boundaries of poetry. In 1967 she won the Pulitzer Prize for her collection *Live or Die.* Three books of her poetry were published after her death.

Varlam Shalamov, 1907–1982, Russian journalist, trained classical poet, and short story writer, published four volumes of poetry, some essays, and translations from Kazakh, Chuvash, Bulgarian, and Yiddish. He is considered one of the greatest writers of Slavic literature.

Edgar Silex, of Pueblo, Hispanic, and European descent, is the author of two poetry collections, *Acts of Love* and *Through All the Displacements.* He teaches at St. Mary's College of Maryland and has received fellowships from the NEA and the Maryland State Arts Council.

Gary Snyder, Zen poet and environmental activist, has worked as a logger and a trail-crew member and studied Asian languages at Berkeley. He has written many books of poetry and prose, including *Turtle Island,* which won the Pulitzer Prize for poetry. He is currently professor of English at the University of California, Davis.

Adam J. Sorkin's translations have appeared widely. Recent volumes include Daniela Crasnaru's *The Grand Prize and Other Stories* and Marin Sorescu's *The Bridge,* which was shortlisted for the biennial Corneliu M. Popescu Prize of the Poetry Society, London. Sorkin received an NEA poetry fellowship for translation for 2005–2006.

Suzanne P. Stetkevych, professor of Arabic literature at Indiana University, Bloomington, is the author of *Abu Tammam and the Poetics of the Abbasid Age, The Mute Immortals Speak: Pre-Islamic Poetry and the Poetics of Ritual,* and *The Poetics of Islamic Legitimacy: Myth, Gender, and Ceremony in the Classical Arabic Ode.* Her research has received support from the Fulbright Foundation, the Social Science Research Council, and the National Endowment for the Humanities.

Wallace Stevens, 1879–1955, worked briefly as a reporter before becoming an attorney in 1904, specializing in investment banking and the insurance business. A lyric poet, in 1946 Stevens was elected to the National Institute of Arts and Letters. He received the Bollingen Prize in poetry and in 1955 was awarded both the Pulitzer Prize and the National Book Award.

May Swenson, 1919–1989, author of eleven books of poetry, one prose work, and two anthologies, had poems published in a variety of magazines. She taught at Bryn Mawr, the University of North Carolina, the University of California, Riverside,

Purdue University, and Utah State University and was an editor at New Directions Publishers from 1959 to 1966. She served as a chancellor of the Academy of American Poets from 1980 to 1989.

Maia Tekses has made several extended trips to the former Austro-Hungarian empire and the former Soviet Union. She has published a few of her translations from central and eastern European languages in small magazines and currently writes under several names and teaches school.

Aleksandr Tkachenko holds a degree in philology and from 1963 to 1970 played professional soccer in Moscow and St. Petersburg. He has published seven volumes of poetry, edited a number of Russian magazines, and was a founding member and general director of the Russian PEN Center. Tkachenko is a member of the executive council of the International Parliament.

Leslie Ullman has authored three poetry collections: *Natural Histories*, which won the Yale Series of Younger Poets Award in 1979, *Dreams by No One's Daughter*, and *Slow Work through Sand*, which was the co-winner of the 1997 Iowa Poetry Prize. She has been awarded two NEA fellowships. Numerous anthologies and magazines have published her poetry, and her poetry reviews have appeared in *Poetry* and the *Kenyon Review*. Ullman directs the MFA program at the University of Texas at El Paso and is on the faculty of the Vermont College MFA Program.

Umayyah Ibn Abi Salt, 1067–1134, was an Islamic poet who extolled moral values and ideals of freedom, justice, valor, and truth.

Mihai Ursachi, 1941–2004, eminent Romanian writer and Nobel Prize nominee in 2001, authored ten poetry collections and a book of short stories. In 1992 he won the first national Mihai Eminescu Poetry Prize to be awarded since World War II.

David Wagoner has published ten novels and seventeen books of poems, most recently *Good Morning and Good Night*. He has won the Ruth Lilly Poetry Prize and numerous other prizes and has been nominated twice for the National Book Award. He was a chancellor of the Academy of American Poets for twenty-three years and is professor emeritus at the University of Washington.

Michael S. Weaver now publishes under the name Afaa Michael Weaver. He spent time on an Arabian horse farm as a child with an uncle who bred, raised, and trained Arabians for show. Weaver's nine books of poetry include *Multitudes, Talisman, My Father's Geography*, and *Timber and Prayer*. He teaches at Simmons College, where he is the chairman of the Simmons International Chinese Poetry Conference.

Claude Wilkinson has produced several poetry collections including *Reading the Earth*, winner of the Naomi Long Madgett Poetry Award, and *Joy in the Morning*. He has

served as the John and Renee Grisham Visiting Southern Writer in Residence at
the University of Mississippi. Other honors include the Walter E. Dakin Fellowship
in poetry and the Whiting Writer's Award.

Nancy Willard teaches at Vassar College and has received grants from the NEA in both
poetry and fiction. Her most recent books include *In the Salt Marsh* and *The Tale of
Paradise Lost*. Her collection of poems for children, *A Visit to William Blake's Inn*,
won the Newbery Medal.

William Carlos Williams, 1883–1963, medical doctor and poet, published short stories,
novels, plays, critical essays, translations, and an autobiography. He was in medical
practice from 1910 to 1951, during which time he authored numerous books of
poetry. He won a Pulitzer Prize in 1963, the National Book Award, and the Gold
Medal for Poetry of the National Institute of Arts and Letters.

James Wright, 1927–1980, won the Yale Series of Younger Poets award in 1957 for his
book *The Green Wall*. He published eleven books of poetry, one volume of collected
prose, and many anthologies of translated works. Wright was elected a fellow of
the Academy of American Poets in 1971, and the following year his *Collected Poems*
received the Pulitzer Prize. He taught at the University of Minnesota, Macalester
College, and New York City's Hunter College.

Xi Chuan, published poet, essayist, and translator since 1985, worked as an editor at
Huanqiu (Globe) magazine before becoming a teacher of English and classical
Chinese literature at the Central Institute of Fine Arts in 1993. He is presently
an editor at the new China News Agency.

Paul Zech, 1881–1946, German poet and writer of prose, worked for two years in
the coal mines and steel mills of the Ruhr, Belgium, and northern France.
He identified with the working class in a spirit of Christian religiosity, vitalism,
and awe of nature. The self-imposed challenge that drove him and his sympathies
emerges in his writings.

Barnett Zumoff is president of the Forward Association, copresident of the Congress
for Jewish Culture, and former president of the Workmen's Circle. His thirteen
books published or in press include translations of Yiddish poetry and prose
and anthologies of both Yiddish and American Yiddish poetry.

Rajzel Zychlinsky, 1910–2001, published her poetry collections *Bread for the Birds—
Five Decades of Poetry* and *Die Gedichter/Die Lider* in German, though she was
Polish. *Lider* was written in Yiddish. *God Hid His Face* is an English translation by
various translators, among them Barnett Zumoff and Zychlinsky's son, Marek
Kanter. She published various other collections. In 1951 Zychlinsky immigrated
to the States, where she continued writing Yiddish poetry until her death.

David Baker, "After Rain," from *Changeable Thunder*, University of Arkansas Press, 2001. Reprinted by permission of the author. "The Judas-Horse," from *Midwest Eclogue*, W. W. Norton and Company, 2005. Reprinted by permission of the author.

Robin Becker, "Phaeton" and sections 2 and 8 from "The Horse Fair," from *The Horse Fair*, copyright © 2000 by Robin Becker. Reprinted by permission of the University of Pittsburgh Press.

Vizma Belševica, "Horses," from *Gada Gredzeni*, ed. Janis Sirmbaardis, 1969, copyright © 1969 by Vizma Belševica. Translation by Ilze Klavina Mueller. Reprinted by permission of Janis Elsbergs (son of Vizma Belševica) and Ilze Klavina Mueller.

Linda Bierds, "The Klipsan Stallions," from *The Stillness, The Dancing*, Henry Holt and Company. Copyright © 1988 by Linda Bierds. Reprinted by permission of the author.

Paul Boldt, "Young Horses! Young Horses!" from *Junge Pferde! Junge Pferde! Das Gesamtwerk: Lyrik, Prosa, Dokumente*, trans. by Ernest Bernhardt-Kabisch. Reprinted by permission of Ernest Bernhardt-Kabisch.

Alison Brackenbury, "After the X-Ray," from *The Poetry of Horses*, J. A. Allen and Company, 1994. Reprinted by permission of Carcanet Press Limited.

Gwendolyn Brooks, "Horses Graze," from *Celebrations: A New Anthology of Black American Poetry*, Follett Publishing Company, copyright © 1977 by Gwendolyn Brooks. Reprinted by permission of Brooks Permissions.

Lucille Clifton, "i once knew a man," copyright © 1980 by Lucille Clifton. First appeared in *Two-Headed Woman*, University of Massachusetts Press. Now appears in *Contemporary American Poetry*, 5th edition. Reprinted by permission of Curtis Brown, Ltd.

Pablo Antonio Cuadra, "Horses in the Lake," translation by Grace Schulman and Ann McCarthy de Zavala, from *Songs of Cifar and the Sweet Sea*, Columbia University Press, and from the *Hudson Review*. Reprinted by permission of Grace Schulman and Ann McCarthy de Zavala.

Babette Deutsch, "Morning Workout," from *The Norton Book of Sports*, W. W. Norton and Company, 1992.

James Dickey, "The Dusk of Horses" and "Horses and Prisoners," from *The Whole Motion: Collected Poems, 1945–1992*, copyright © 1992 by James Dickey. Reprinted by permission of Wesleyan University Press.

Stephen Dobyns, "The Triangular Field," from *Velocities*, copyright © 1994 by Stephen Dobyns. Reprinted by permission of Penguin, a division of Penguin Group (USA).

Kay Ryan, "Grazing Horses," from *Say Uncle*, Grove Press, copyright © 2000 by Kay Ryan. Reprinted by permission of the author.

Carl Sandburg, "Horses and Men in Rain," from *Cornhuskers* by Carl Sandburg, copyright © 1918 by Holt, Rinehart and Winston and renewed 1946 by Carl Sandburg. Reprinted by permission of Harcourt.

May Sarton, "The Horse-Pulling," from *Collected Poems 1930–1993*, copyright © 1993, 1988, 1984, 1980, 1974 by May Sarton. Used by permission of W. W. Norton and Company.

Anne Sexton, "Horse," from *45 Mercy Street*, ed. Linda Gray Sexton, copyright © 1976 by Linda Gray Sexton and Loring Conant, Jr., executors of the estate of Anne Sexton. Reprinted by permission of Houghton Mifflin Company and SLL/Sterling Lord Literistic, Inc.

Varlam Shalamov, "Pegasus," trans. Bradley Jordan, from *20th Century Russian Poetry* by Yevgeny Yevtushenko, copyright © 1993 by Doubleday. Used by permission of Doubleday, a division of Random House.

Edgar Silex, "Blue Cloud Rides Horses," from *Poetry Like Bread*, Curbstone Press, 1994. Reprinted by permission of the author.

Gary Snyder, "All through the Rains," from *Riprap and Cold Mountain Poems*, copyright © 2004 by Gary Snyder. Reprinted by permission of Shoemaker and Hoard.

Wallace Stevens, "Polo Ponies Practicing," from *Collected Poems of Wallace Stevens*, copyright © 1954 by Wallace Stevens. Reprinted by permission of Alfred A. Knopf, a division of Random House.

"Stewball," an old Irish folksong, is taken from a printed version that appeared in an American songbook dated 1829.

May Swenson, "Bronco Busting, Event #1," from *Poems Old and New*, copyright © 1994 by the literary estate of May Swenson. Reprinted by permission of Houghton Mifflin Company.

Aleksandr Tkachenko, "Battle," trans. Maia Tekses, from *In the Grip of Strange Thoughts: Russian Poetry in a New Era*, selected and edited by J. Kates, copyright © 1999 by Zephyr Press.

Leslie Ullman, "Dawn Feeding," from *Dreams by No One's Daughter*, copyright © 1987 by Leslie Ullman. Reprinted by permission of the University of Pittsburgh Press.

Umayyah Ibn Abi Salt, "The White Stallion," translated by Cola Franzen, is taken from *Poems of Arab Andalusia*, City Lights Books, San Francisco, copyright ©1989 by Cola Franzen. Reprinted by permission of Cola Franzen.

Mihai Ursachi, "The Thunder of Silence," reprinted by permission of Archpriest Gheorghe Ursache, literary heir to the rights of the poems of his brother Mihai